EASY WAYS TO GOOD

FLOWER ARRANGEMENT

THE STUDIO PUBLICATIONS, INC. IN ASSOCIATION WITH

MARY BADHAM KITTEL

EASY

WAYS

TO GOOD

FLOWER
ARRANGEMENT

distributed by
FREDERICK MULLER LTD
LONDON

THOMAS Y. CROWELL COMPANY, LONDON & NEW YORK

Designed by EMIL SILVESTRI

Manufactured in the United States of America

Library of Congress Catalog Card No. 57-9253

Third Printing, October 1958

ACKNOWLEDGMENTS

The author wishes to thank the authors and publishers for permission
to use photographs from the following publications: *Christmas Lighting
and Decorating* by Theodore Saros, D. Van Nostrand Company, Inc.;
Garden Glories, official publication of The Garden Club of Illinois, Inc.;
Holiday Flower Arrangements by Emma H. Cyphers, Hearthside Press,
Inc.; and *The National Gardener*, bulletin of The National Council of
State Garden Clubs, Inc.

The author is also grateful to Lawrence Joseph, Bob Maulsby, Anthony
Stoker, Herbert Reid, and Frank Karr for their patience and expert help
on art work; to Marion Tucker, Adel Beavers, and Hope Montanez for
invaluable help in preparing the manuscript; and to Esther Wheeler,
Lelia McKnight, and Inez Hamilton for expert guidance and inspiration
throughout the past ten years.

CONTENTS

ONE

THREE FLOWERS AND A CONTAINER

MAXIMUM EFFECT WITH MINIMUM MATERIAL AND EFFORT
MAY BE OBTAINED BY THE SKILLFUL ARRANGEMENT OF
only three flowers.

With a little study the rankest amateur can learn to conserve valuable time and money by making three flowers take the place of a dozen. Once mastered, the design principles governing their placement may be applied to the most complex arrangement.

As has been said many times, it is not *what* you arrange, but *how* you arrange it that tells the story.

PLATE 1.

The three-point arrangement of irises in Plate 1 is an adaptation from the Japanese. It involves measurements that are easy to follow. Even those who "simply cannot make an arrangement" may use the mathematical formula given in the accompanying drawings and produce pleasing results.

The irises have been arranged in accordance with their natural habit of growth to simulate a single plant. They could actually be growing from the black pebbles that are used to cover the needlepoint holder. In addition to helping create a poolside effect, the pebbles blend with the dark bronze container in both color and texture. They look much more natural than iris leaves wrapped around the holder, or stems cut to fill unused portions of needles. Instead of being an obvious makeshift, the pebbles actually *add* to the design.

A study of nature will prove most helpful in solving the problem of concealing mechanics. Material that *belongs* on the ground—things that would normally be found in this position—are best for use at the base of an arrangement. Moss, lichens, stones, or small pieces of weathered wood are ideal. A little imagination will reveal many interesting substitutes.

The two teakwood stands which have been placed under the container in Plate 1 add much importance to this simple design. Stands not only give stability, but often change the entire feeling of an arrangement. A collection of stands, or bases, will prove a stimulating and worthwhile investment. Effects achieved by trying out various sizes and shapes will teach the designer a great deal about balance and proportion—two very important factors in any design.

Experience will show that when two stands of a set are used, the best visual balance is obtained by combining the largest stand of a set with the next-to-smallest, and the smallest stand with the next-to-largest.

The following step-by-step notes on how the first arrangement was made may be clarified by referring to Plate 1 and Drawing I.

1. Since the bronze container and dark stands in Plate 1 gave a feeling of great stability, and the irises were all the same size, the one with the longest stem was selected for the main line. If a bud had been available it would have been used in the first position.

2. Cut the stem of the flower selected for the main line from one and a half to five times as long as container is high (depending upon the visual weight of the container and material). The taller the arrangement the more drama it will have; however, too much height will make the design appear top-heavy. An arrangement that looks as if it might topple over usually *will* topple over; and even if it does not, the lack of visual balance will prove disconcerting.

3. Place the longest iris in the center of the holder, in the position indicated on diagram A (Drawing I). Be sure that the tip of the flower is immediately over the base of the stem. No matter how crooked the stem may be, balance is more easily achieved if the tip of the central

PLATE 1 ►

flower is immediately over the point where the stem is attached to the needlepoint holder. The stem of the iris used here happened to be fairly straight, but this principle would apply regardless of how crooked the stem might be.

4. Select the next longest iris (if there is a choice, save the largest bloom for last position), and cut the stem two thirds the height of the first flower.

5. Referring to diagram A (Drawing I), place bloom #2 immediately behind first blossom, so that it clings to stem #1 for at least three inches and then reaches out toward back of container. For best results, bloom should attain a thirty-degree angle and reach out over lip of container between points 7 and 8 on diagram A. It should look up toward first iris, *not* bow to the floor.

6. Cut the stem of the largest, most perfect flower two thirds the length of iris #2.

7. Place this iris immediately in front of #1. Have it cling to the other stems at the base and start reaching out just below point where #2 leaves the main stem. This bloom will be more effective if it attains a forty-five-degree angle and reaches out over the lip of the container between points 3 and 4 on diagram A. The lower iris, while looking up to the first flower, should point toward the observer's right shoulder.

8. Iris leaves may be added in front of, and behind, the tallest iris, to strengthen the main line. No two leaves should be exactly the same height.

9. Iris #2 should be strengthened in the same manner, but leaves should not droop below the blossom and spoil the clarity of line.

10. Iris #3 should be strengthened with the remaining leaves; but nothing should fall below the flower, as it might confuse the lower line.

11. One iris leaf may be bent so that it will reach out over lip of container between points 1 and 2 on diagram A. Japanese arrangers break or bend this leaf, indicating that nothing in nature is perfect, or that a bird rested there a moment and has just flown away.

Even to those not in a fanciful mood, the leaf serves a definite purpose, for it adds depth to the arrangement. The flower arranger in creating a picture is not limited, as the painter is, to two dimensions—height and width. Our medium, like the sculptor's, has the advantage of depth; much distinction is added through emphasizing this factor. No arrangement should end with a flat façade, regardless of its function. To realize the full beauty of a flower or an arrangement, look *into* it, not *at* it.

12. A final check of the completed arrangement should show the tip of the tallest iris immediately over the base of the stem, all stems cling-

DIAGRAM - B   DIAGRAM - C

PLATE NO. 1   PLATE NO. 2

Drawing I, to be referred to while reading step-by-step procedures for making arrangements shown in Plates 1, 2, 3.

ing closely together for at least 3 inches at the bottom of the design, and the three flowers looking toward the sun in a naturalistic manner (see diagram B).

PLATE 2.

The same container and stands shown in Plate 1 were used in Plate 2. Peonies were substituted for the irises, and the position of the two lower flowers was reversed.

Three small cypress knees cover the needlepoint holder, helping to create the illusion of a single peony plant growing from an old, gnarled stump. Again the device used to cover mechanics, instead of being a makeshift, actually contributes to the design.

If cypress knees are soaked in warm water overnight, the bark can be worked loose at the cut end and peeled off very easily. After the bark was removed from the three small knees, they were rubbed with brown shoe polish until they took on the texture and coloring of the bronze container.

1. Select the peony with the longest, most interesting stem for central placement. As with the irises, the stem for the main placement should be from one and a half to five times the height of container. Although height lends drama, the visual weight of the container and stands, as well as of the plant material, governs the feeling of stability. If a bud had been available for this first position, instead of a heavy flower, more height could have been achieved without a top-heavy effect.

2. Place the longest stem in the center of the holder, in the position indicated on diagram A (Drawing I), checking to be sure the tip of the flower falls immediately over the base of the stem. In order to take full advantage of an interestingly curved stem, the peony shown in Plate 2 was turned slowly in the hand until the most effective profile was determined. After the stem was impaled on the needlepoint holder so that the curve showed to best advantage, the flower was tilted toward the back of the container until the tip of the blossom fell immediately over the place where the stem left the holder.

3. Select the next bloom (saving the largest flower for the last position) and cut the stem two thirds the height of the first peony. The flower used in the photograph had a very crooked stem, which makes it appear

PLATE 2 ►

somewhat foreshortened. A more pleasing effect would have been achieved had the second placement, together with its supporting leaf, been a few inches higher.

4. Impale blossom #2 immediately behind the first stem, so that both stems cling together for at least three inches. The flower should then reach out toward back of container between points 2 and 3 on diagram A (Drawing I), with the blossom looking up toward the first peony.

5. Next, select the largest, most perfect bloom and, allowing for curves, cut the stem two thirds the length of peony #2.

6. Place this bloom immediately in front of #1, with the stem clinging to the other two stems at the base and leaning forward just below the point where #2 leaves the main stem. This flower should reach out over the lip of the container between points 5 and 6 on diagram A, looking up and pointing over the arranger's left shoulder.

7. Leaves may be added to strengthen all three lines and to give depth. However, placements should vary in height, not only with each other, but with the leaves and blossoms already included in the design.

8. A final check should show the tip of the main flower immediately over the cut end of the stem, all stems clinging closely together for at least three inches, and the three flowers looking toward the sun in a naturalistic manner (see diagram C, Drawing I).

PLATE 3.

A tall, square, pottery container on a single stand is shown in Plate 3. Again three bold flowers have been arranged to give maximum effect.

These striking flowers, though comparatively expensive, are an excellent buy because the blooms stay fresh for ten days or two weeks. Strelitzia (bird of paradise) foliage is almost as dramatic as the brilliantly colored flowers, but it is difficult to buy. Cutting the leaves weakens the plant, and weight makes shipping so high that leaves are often as expensive as blossoms.

Strelitzia leaves were not available when arrangement shown here was made, so other foliage had to be substituted. Amaryllis leaves, which have somewhat the texture and coloring of the strelitzia stems, helped achieve the desired effect.

Arrangers striving for naturalistic groupings will find familiarity with

PLATE 3 ►

the growing habits of foliage a great help. There is a definite back and front to all foliage. The veining is usually more prominent on the back of the leaf—the side that faces the earth or *away* from the central stalk. The Japanese call the side of the leaf that faces the sun the male side; and the side that looks toward the earth, the female side. They never make the mistake of showing the male side of leaf with a downward look, nor do they allow the female side to have heavenly aspirations.

1. The most interestingly shaped stem was selected for tallest placement. The flower was impaled in the center of the needlepoint holder with the lip of the bloom pointing between 3 and 4 on diagram A (Drawing I), between the right and front corners of the container.

2. The second bloom was cut two thirds the length of bloom #1 and attached to the holder immediately behind #1, with the flower pointing toward #3 on diagram A—toward the right-hand corner of the container.

3. The lowest blossom was cut two thirds the length of #2 and placed on the holder immediately in front of #1, swinging it behind the curved stem of #2 to point between 2 and 3 on diagram A—between the right-hand and back corners of the container. (If the stem for #2 had been straight, #3 would have pointed to 4 on diagram A, rather than toward the back of the container.)

4. Amaryllis leaves were grouped around the three stems, to give the effect of a single unit. All leaves face each other around the central axis, as if growing from a single bulb, and each of the three groups of leaves was cut two thirds the length of the preceding one. Care was exercised to see that the leaves varied in height with each other, as well as with the three blossoms.

5. A final check was made to see that nothing had been added which might confuse the three original placements and that the leaves had been kept short enough to reveal the beauty of strelitzia stems. Since most amaryllis bloom stalks are well developed before the leaves appear, nature was not violated in shortening the foliage.

PLATE 4.

The simple arrangement of calla lilies in a Swedish glass bowl, shown in Plate 4, gains elegance and importance through the use of an interesting stand. Again, with only a slight change in placement, a natural-

PLATE 4 ▶

istic grouping of three flowers has been used to obtain maximum effect.

Glass containers are often a problem. The water distorts stems, and the design below the water is as important as the design above water. Stems should be arranged to enhance the beauty of the container, and great care should be taken in covering mechanics. The glass slag used in this design, by emphasizing distortion, lends distinction to the composition and seems to be a part of the bowl itself. The stems of both flowers and leaves were manipulated to repeat the graceful curve of the container.

Although three flowers of the same size may be used effectively, it is much easier to create the illusion of a growing plant with blooms in varying stages of development. The three callas were identical, as is usually the case with material from the florist. Variation in size was achieved by using only the middle bloom as it came from the florist. The top flower was squeezed back into bud form, and overlapping edges were Scotch-Taped *on the inside* to prevent opening. The lower calla was forced wider open and split slightly near the stem, to prevent the flower from returning to its original size.

The white portion of calla stems should be removed in order to assure proper water absorption and prolong the life of blooms. This procedure is advisable in arranging any flower with similar growing habits.

Calla foliage should be allowed to harden in a tub of water to which a handful of baking soda has been added. It will last for two weeks or longer if properly conditioned, but untreated foliage wilts very quickly. Leaves should be weighted down with a bath towel, or anything soft enough to hold them under water without bruising, and kept submerged for at least two hours—preferably overnight. Both yellow and white calla foliage is well worth the trouble and will outlast the blooms if properly treated. *Any* foliage hardened in this manner will last longer.

Calla stems are obligingly pliable; with care they may be gently massaged into almost any desired curve. A No. 8 wire run through the center of the stem, before the bending process is started, will guarantee lasting results. The wire cannot be seen, and it does not affect the life of the bloom.

Callas, amaryllis, and other heavy blooms with fleshy stems are apt to give trouble unless cut ends of stems are reinforced before being placed on the needlepoint holder. Stem ends should be wrapped with Floraltape, Scotch Tape, string, or rubber bands. If further reinforcement is necessary, a small, two-inch length of willow, ligustrum, or any woody shrub, may be forced into the cut end (see diagram A, Drawing II). This may be done either before or after the stem is wrapped and will hold even the heaviest blossom firmly in place.

1. The smallest blossom should be selected for the main line and the stem cut above the white portion. The calla stems were not long enough to make them appear top-heavy, so maximum length was allowed in the first placement. The cut end was wrapped to keep it from splitting and the stem gently massaged until it followed the desired curve.

2. Impale stem #1 on left back of holder, in the position indicated on diagram B (Drawing II). The tip of the flower should fall immediately over spot where the stem is attached to the needlepoint holder, with the lip of the blossom pointing toward 3 on diagram B.

3. Select the next-sized blossom (saving the largest calla for the last position) and cut the stem two thirds the length of first bloom. Bend the stem gently until it follows the curve of stem #1. After wrapping the bottom of the stem to keep it from splitting, place the flower immediately in front of stem #1, in the position indicated on diagram B. Blossom #2 should follow the curve of #1 with the lip of the flower pointing between 2 and 3 on diagram B.

4. Since the stem of the largest blossom will be quite curved, it should be cut only a little shorter than #2.

5. After wrapping stem #3 to keep it from splitting, force a No. 8 wire from the cut end up into the bloom head.

6. Hold flower #3 in the position indicated by the photograph and, after determining the line that the stem should follow, gently massage it into desired curve. This flower should hug the other two stems and curve around them, reaching out over the edge of the container between points 4 and 5 on diagram B.

7. Place the largest calla leaf behind blossom #1. It should be slightly shorter than the flower, and the leaf stem should follow the curve of bloom stem.

8. Place a smaller leaf in front of #2, slightly shorter than the second flower and following its curve.

9. Select a larger leaf to support blossom #3. This leaf should be slightly *longer* than the blossom, following the curve of the flower stem and reaching out over the edge of the container between points 4 and 5 on diagram B.

10. Additional small leaves may be incorporated at center of the design if needed to help create the illusion of a growing plant. The largest leaves should form the outside of the design, enclosing the smaller leaves at the center.

11. A final check should show leaves varying in height with each other and with the three flowers; all leaves looking up toward the sun and facing in toward the center of growth.

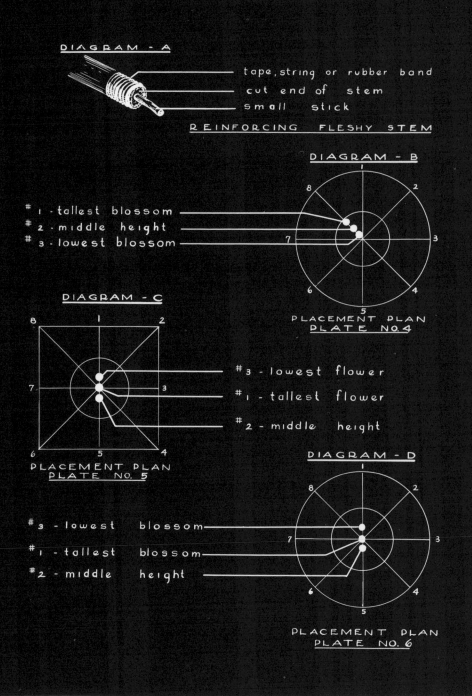

DIAGRAM - A

tape, string or rubber band
cut end of stem
small stick

REINFORCING   FLESHY   STEM

DIAGRAM - B

1 - tallest blossom
2 - middle height
3 - lowest blossom

PLACEMENT PLAN
PLATE NO. 4

DIAGRAM - C

#3 - lowest flower
#1 - tallest flower
#2 - middle height

PLACEMENT PLAN
PLATE NO. 5

DIAGRAM - D

#3 - lowest blossom
#1 - tallest blossom
#2 - middle height

PLACEMENT PLAN
PLATE NO. 6

Drawing II, with diagrams for Plates 4, 5, and 6.

PLATE 5.

Three daffodils in a low, black, pottery container lined with chartreuse are shown in Plate 5. Again the container has been placed on a base to add importance to the simple design, and again self foliage helps create the illusion of a growing plant. The dull black lava rocks covering the needlepoint holder repeat the texture and coloring of the container and, at the same time, add stability to the design.

The secret of obtaining maximum effect from three daffodils, or other plants with similar growth habits, lies in the naturalistic grouping of foliage. The leaves grow so compactly against the bloom stem that flower and foliage must be placed in the holder as a unit. Even leaves that do not actually support a flower should be carefully grouped before being placed in the container.

Each flower should be surrounded by three or four leaves of varying heights, all facing toward the central stem, as if they were growing from a single bulb. The stems may be held together with Floraltape, string, Scotch Tape, or elastic bands. These aids can be concealed after the groups have been placed in the container.

The hollow flower stems are easily wired and can be made to stay in any position. If juice (or latex) from the end of the bloom stem is rubbed on both sides of the foliage, it too can be persuaded to hold almost any curve.

After having been hardened in deep water overnight—or for at least two hours—most bulbous plants will live out their full life span in very shallow water.

1. Select the tallest, most upright daffodil. After cutting the stem above the white portion, group three leaves of varying height around it and secure them together as a unit. The proportion of the leaves to the blossom in this group sets the pattern for the other placements. If the leaves reach above the bloom, other groups should follow suit. If they fall below the flower, those in the other units should also fall below the flower.

Oriental arrangers make daffodil leaves shorter than the blossoms in early spring and longer than the flowers as the season advances, since this is the way they would normally grow in the garden.

2. Place the tallest flower in the center of the needlepoint holder with the tip of the trumpet immediately over the point where the stem is attached to the holder. The trumpet should face the edge of the container between points 3 and 4 on diagram C (Drawing II).

3. Group the leaves, which have been softened with latex, around the

stem of the middle-sized bloom and cut the unit two thirds the height of #1.

4. Impale this unit on the holder in the position indicated on diagram C (Drawing II). The second group should cling to #1 for at least two inches and then lean out toward the back of the container, between points 7 and 8 on diagram C, with the bloom looking up toward the first flower. If the leaves are moistened and stroked gently between thumb and forefinger they will curve gracefully and may be made to follow the direction you desire them to take. One leaf tip may point toward the first blossom and one toward the lip of the container between points 7 and 8, while the third leaf clings to the bloom stem.

5. Moisten the leaves of the lowest unit (largest flower) and run No. 8 wire through the bloom stem. Since this group will be quite curved, it should be cut only slightly shorter than #2. After placement, however, the unit should *appear* to be two thirds the height of #2.

6. Impale this group on the holder in the position indicated on diagram C, bending the stems so that they curve around the other two groups, hugging them closely and swinging out over the front of the container between 4 and 5 on diagram C. The trumpet should point toward bloom #1, and each leaf should be stroked until it follows the curve of the wired blossom. These leaves may reach out toward the lip of the container anywhere between 3 and 5, or one of them may swing up and point toward first bloom.

7. Several groups of leaves may be added to strengthen the three placements and to emphasize the feeling of growth.

8. A final check should show all units made up of leaves which vary in length and face each other around a central axis, regardless of whether they surround a flower stem or are grouped alone. All groups should show the tallest leaf longer than the bloom, or all should be shorter than the bloom. Only material actually necessary to the design should be used; if in doubt about a group, remove it. One of the greatest attributes of beauty in any art is simplicity.

PLATE 5 ►

PLATE 6.

Even the formality of the gladiolus lends itself to the simplicity of a three-point design. Properly arranged, three of these dignified blooms will give more drama to a room than three dozen stalks arranged in the usual manner.

Plate 6 shows a different kind of Japanese usubata from the one shown in Plates 1 and 2. The distinguishing feature of a usubata is the flaring, saucerlike top with a built-in flange, or well, for holding water. They come in many sizes and a variety of shapes, and the tops are usually removable. Orientals fill only the well, or flange, with water during the dry season, while arrangements made during the rainy season show the entire top flooded with water.

The container depicted here is fairly massive in itself and looks better with only one base, while the usubata in Plates 1 and 2, even though it is used with much lighter flowers, requires the added stability given by two stands.

Exactly the same procedure used for the daffodils in Plate 5 was followed in arranging the gladioli, except that extra leaves were not grouped with the flowers before incorporating them into the design.

The well of the container was so narrow and deep that it did not require additional material to hide the holder. However, either the pebbles used in preceding plates or the cypress knees shown in Plate 2 would have been suitable had the design needed extra weight at the base.

Tapering tips or buds of gladioli and other similar plants should be disregarded when measuring proposed height for an arrangement. Measurement starts just above the first fully opened floret and ends above the portion of stem which will be concealed by the container.

Since additional foliage is often needed, leaves should be carefully preserved when cutting gladioli stems. The leaf encasing the stem where the cut is to be made should be pulled away from the stalk and the stem cut beneath the foliage. If all cuts are made in this manner there will usually be foliage to spare.

1. Select the two gladioli stalks with smallest number of open florets. The number of florets which are fully open usually varies slightly, even in uniform florist gladioli; and the stalk with either the fewest or the

PLATE 6 ►

next-to-fewest open flowers may be used for the first placement. The deciding factor should be the interesting shape of stem or tip.

This first placement is the *backbone* of the arrangement. *It is by far the most important line in the composition.*

2. Disregarding the bud tip, and allowing for the depth of the container, cut the chosen stem from one and a half to five times the height of the container. Turn the stem to determine most interesting profile and place the stalk on the center of the needlepoint holder. The bloom should be twisted gently until it faces between 5 and 6 on diagram D (Drawing II).

3. Pull the lower leaf back and cut the second stalk two thirds the height of blossom #1. Place on the needlepoint holder in the position shown on diagram D, with florets looking up toward blossom #1. The bud tip should be stroked gently until it reaches toward the first placement, and the stalk should lean toward the back of the container between 7 and 8 on diagram D.

The sparsest bloom is often used by Orientals in the back placement, which they consider north (development would naturally be slower in a northern exposure). The real purpose of the placement is to add depth. Sparseness increases the illusion of distance, and this emphasizes the sculptural quality so necessary to a good flower arrangement.

4. The fullest bloom, or rather the stalk with greatest number of open florets, should be selected for the lowest position. Since this stem will be quite curved, it should be cut only slightly shorter than #2. (It can always be shortened later if necessary.)

5. Place gladiolus #3 on a flat, firm surface and carefully work a wire as far up the stem as possible. If the wire cannot be forced the whole way up the stem, the process may be repeated from the blossom end. Starting beneath the second or third bud, work another wire carefully through the stalk until it overlaps the first wire.

6. Place the stem on the holder in the position indicated on diagram D. After determining the line the stalk must follow, massage the stem gently until it curves around the other placements and reaches out over the lip of the container between 3 and 4 on diagram D. The flower should look up toward bloom #1.

7. Trim foliage and group it together in natural-looking pairs, before strengthening the three placements.

8. A final check should show all blossoms looking up toward the sun and no light showing through the base of the arrangement. Additional foliage should be added so the arrangement gives the illusion of a single plant growing compactly together at the base and spreading above in a naturalistic manner.

SUMMARY

1. Everything from the common field daisy (and its sophisticated cousin the gerbera) on up through roses, majestic torch ginger, and giant anthurium, will lend itself to a three-point arrangement. The projects given on the preceding pages show only a few variations in placement. Infinite variety is possible.
2. The more closely natural habits of growth are followed, the simpler it will be to create a pleasing effect.
3. The tallest placement should appear to be young growth springing vigorously from the center of the plant and reaching toward the light. The lowest stem should look as if it had been pulled downward by the weight of the maturer bloom (which still looks up toward the sun).
4. Stems should cling together at the base of the arrangement. There should be three distinct planes giving *depth,* but the flowers should appear to be a single plant growing from a central axis. Visualize a triangular cornucopia attached by its tip to the holder — *not* a flat, open fan.
5. Three flowers in different stages of development are easier to arrange than three blooms of identical size.
6. Except when using heavy, woody material, stems should be recut each time they are placed on the holder. The fresh cut will assure a firm footing and minimize the danger of the flowers slipping out of place.
7. Slender containers, or those giving the effect of fragility, often look better with two bases.
8. Height lends drama. Arrangements are more effective if they are made as tall as the visual weight of the container and material will allow. The heavier the flowers, and the more they flare out from the central stem, the more visual weight is required at the base of the design.
9. Arbitrary rules set down by Oriental flower arrangers are usually based on good, sound design factors. Even those not interested in the symbolism entailed in the material and its placement will profit by studying any of the Japanese books listed in glossary.
10. With a well-chosen container and stands, *any* three properly arranged flowers may become eye catchers, regardless of the size of the room.

Those who develop a seeing eye through studying nature, and practice making three-point arrangements with various types of flowers, containers, and stands, will become designers in spite of themselves!

THREE PLUS TWO

A FIVE-POINT ARRANGEMENT IS JUST AS EASY TO CONSTRUCT
AS A THREE-FLOWER DESIGN. IT MAY HAPPILY INCORPORATE
five blossoms of the same variety; or, as in Plate 7, it may be a simple
three-point arrangement plus two placements of unrelated material.

A well-chosen branch with three suitable flowers at its feet can play
an important part in any decorative scheme.

PLATE 7.

The oak branches and three yellow tulips in Plate 7 are shown in an
unglazed brown pottery container lined with burnt orange. The brown
and orange rocks used to cover the holder help create a naturalistic
effect and add necessary weight at the base of the design. The solid
dark base beneath the container gives visual stability and keeps the
small receptacle from seeming inadequate for the heavy branches. The
block was fashioned from mill ends and looks as if it had been made
for the container. Their affinity, however, is purely coincidental. The

container takes on an entirely different character when used with other bases, and the block is equally happy with any one of a half-dozen containers.

The branch in Plate 7 was a source of constantly changing beauty for weeks. It turned from the dormant branch shown here, into one with swelling leaf nodules; produced chartreuse catkins; and finally tiny flame-colored leaves appeared. Following the life cycle of the oak, violets, snowdrops, cyclamen, grape hyacinths, jonquils, yard-grown tulips and yellow roses were placed at its feet. At Christmas time the branch was glitter-flecked and wore gold stars in its hair. The flowers were replaced with a chunky red candle which burned as a center of interest throughout the holidays.

Dormant branches brought into the house early in January pay big dividends. Contrary to common opinion they do *not* have to be flowering shrubs. Even the most ordinary tree or shrub will prove worthwhile. Oak, cottonwood, elm, chinaberry, soapberry, pecan, hickory, horse chestnut, maple, alder, haw, crabapple, etc., are even more gratifying than prize flowering shrubs.

Properly handled branches not only put out catkins (or blossoms, as the case may be), but after the catkins fall produce miniature leaves in the most unbelievable colors. Fully matured cottonwood catkins (which ordinarily grow too high to be really appreciated) are as big as a man's thumb. They turn vivid purple during one stage of development!

A month-early spring may be obtained by giving branches a warm shower once a week, then crushing the stem ends and placing them in a water-filled container. Making the warm bath a daily process will often speed up development even more.

Dormant branches respond best to baths which give them the feel of drenching spring rains. The easiest procedure is to place branches in an empty bathtub (with drain closed) and allow the shower to run very gently. The drain should be opened as soon as the tub is filled and branches should be removed after the tub is empty.

Prolonged soaking tends to waterlog the buds and may cause discoloration or rot; handling branches while they are heavy with water may bruise or break the tender buds. Branches should not, therefore, remain submerged and should be allowed to drain (but not dry out) before being transferred back to the container. Soaking branches is only necessary to keep bark soft enough for buds to break through, so baths may be discontinued as soon as the buds seem sufficiently swollen to open. However, gentle showers may be given even after blooms appear. (Flower arrangers' families soon learn to spend January and February fighting for a place in the bathtub with redbud, et al!)

32

Branches for forcing should be carefully selected since they must be the proper shape for a designated spot. They may be thinned out or trimmed as desired; but, if the life cycle is to continue, the material should not be twisted or bent in any way. Manipulation injures the buds and slows up or entirely stops development processes.

The pale yellow tulips in Plate 7 were forced indoors expressly for the purpose of completing such an arrangement. Growing flowers for similar designs is a challenge and can be real fun. The entire family will soon become interested in a kitchen window garden and through this interest acquire much valuable horticultural knowledge.

Long stems are not necessary in these midwinter designs and quick bloom is essential. A hundred-watt bulb kept burning immediately above the tulip pot at night, and on dark days, speeds development. (Conversely, if yard-grown tulips show a tendency to bloom too close to the ground, they should be kept in the dark. An empty flower pot turned upside down over the short-stemmed buds will make them reach upward — looking for light — before proceeding with the opening process.)

The five-point placement plan used in Plate 7 is exceedingly versatile and easy to follow. However, the ends of heavy branches which are to be used on needlepoint holders require special treatment. The ends of the tough oak branches in the photograph were pounded with a hammer for an inch or two. The hammered ends were then crisscrossed with half-inch-deep cuts, made with a knife, so they would be soft enough to impale on the holder.

Breaking down the cellulose structure of heavy stem ends is essential, regardless of the type of arrangement. In addition to making the stems easy to place on the holder, it assures proper water absorption. The process should be repeated each time a branch is shortened.

1. A needlepoint holder large enough to carry the heavy branches was placed near the back corner of the square container.

2. The tall branch was turned slowly in the hand to determine its most pleasing profile. It was then placed on the center back of the holder as indicated on diagram A (Drawing III), with the desired line facing the arranger. After being firmly attached to the holder, the branch was tilted toward the back of the container until its tip fell immediately over the point where the stem was attached to the holder.

3. The small branch was then held in varying positions until the most pleasing angle and length was determined.

4. After being shortened to the required length, the end of the branch

was pounded with a hammer and crisscrossed with half-inch cuts so it could be easily placed on the holder and would then absorb the water properly.

5. The second branch was then impaled on the needlepoint holder as near to the first placement as possible. It was tilted forward to the position shown in Plate 7, reaching out over the edge of the container between right and front corner.

6. The tallest tulip was selected for the first placement beneath the branches.

7. The overlapping petals of tulip #1 were Scotch-Taped on the inside to make it retain bud form, in the same manner as the calla lily in Plate 4 was taped. Two leaves of different lengths were then added to the bloom, and the stems were held together as outlined for daffodils in Plate 5.

8. Tulip #1 was placed on the holder as close to the tallest oak branch as possible, in the position shown on diagram A (Drawing III), with its stem and longest leaf following the curve of the branch.

9. The stem of tulip #2 was cut two thirds the length of #1; and, after the leaves were added, the group was placed on the holder immediately in front and to the right of tulip #1. The bloom stem and tallest leaf follow the curve of the lower branch and lean toward the back of the container.

10. The largest tulip was given supporting leaves; and, after being cut two thirds the length of tulip #2, the stem was impaled on the holder as close as possible to the two other groups. The stem follows the curve of the lowest shoot on the small oak branch and reaches out toward the arranger's left shoulder.

11. The crossing shoots of the oak branches were trimmed out. Shoots which drooped toward the floor instead of reaching up toward the sun (as they would if growing in the garden) were also removed.

12. Several groups of tulip leaves were added to create visual weight at the base of the composition and equalize the thrust of the tall oak branch.

13. Rocks were grouped to cover the unused needles and to complete the design.

14. A final check showed the tip of the main line immediately over the point where the branch was impaled on holder and the tulips growing among the rocks in a naturalistic manner.

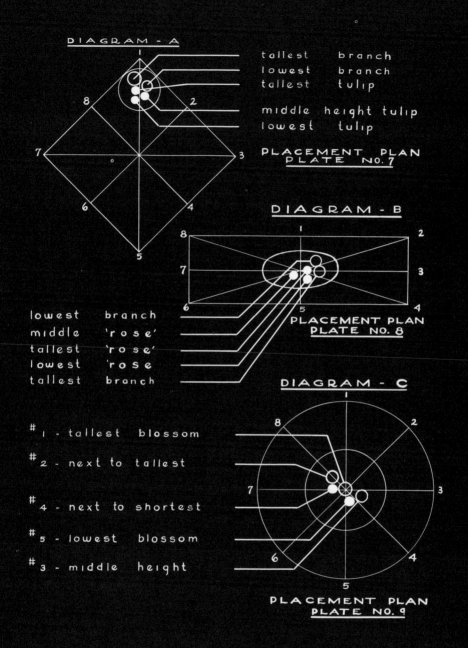

DIAGRAM - A

tallest   branch
lowest   branch
tallest   tulip

middle   height tulip
lowest   tulip

PLACEMENT   PLAN
PLATE   No. 7

DIAGRAM - B

PLACEMENT PLAN
PLATE   NO. 8

lowest   branch
middle   'r o s e'
tallest   'r o s e'
lowest   'r o s e
tallest   branch

#1 - tallest   blossom

#2 - next to tallest

#4 - next to shortest

#5 - lowest   blossom

#3 - middle   height

DIAGRAM - C

PLACEMENT PLAN
PLATE No. 9

Drawing III, with diagrams for Plates 7, 8, and 9.

PLATE 8.

Wild plum brought into the house in early February and given a daily warm shower for several weeks will burst into bloom, permeating the surroundings with exotic perfume. Counterbalancing the forward thrust of the heavy branch shown in Plate 8 are three dark green "roses." The "roses" were made by rolling one galax leaf tightly and wrapping other leaves more loosely around the tightly rolled central leaf. Two of the "roses" were made of five leaves and one was made of seven leaves, to simulate varying size blossoms. Green Floraltape holds each of the groups together, and it is a simple matter to achieve height by adding stems to the "roses" as needed.

Galax leaves are an excellent buy, since they are practically indestructible. If treated with glycerine (see Appendix, item 11) they will turn purple after the first few weeks, remain pliable, and last indefinitely. Violet leaves and geranium leaves make equally lovely "roses," but they do not have the lasting quality of galax. Ivy leaves last fairly well but do not have quite so pleasing a form.

The five-point arrangement of galax leaves and wild plum shown in Plate 8 follows the same placement as preceding plate. However, the position of branches has been reversed as shown on diagram B (Drawing III). The "roses," instead of following line of branches, were placed more closely together than the tulips. This compact grouping was necessary in order to compensate for the heavier forward thrust of the plum branch and the visual weight of its blossoms as compared to the weight of the bare oak branch.

The container in Plate 8 was made by a teen-ager in a home hobby shop. It required nothing but a two-foot section of copper pipe, a little solder, and imagination. The stand was made for an antique bronze usubata, but it seems to complement almost any type of container. A well-chosen stand will often lift very inexpensive containers into unexpected refinement. In addition to giving necessary weight to the design, the stand in Plate 8 makes the copper-pipe container appear handsome enough for the most elegant room!

The needlepoint holder supporting the plum branch is concealed by brown "rose rocks" from Texas. These rocks can be found in all sizes, and look exactly like hand-carved roses. They are particularly effective

PLATE 8 ▶

here, since their color repeats the color of the copper container and their form repeats the shape of the galax clusters.

When the plum blossoms in the photograph fell and tiny green leaves appeared, the galax "roses" were replaced, first with pansies and then with small bunches of violets, surrounded by self-foliage.

Both violets and pansies drink through their heads, and the blossoms must be kept moist in order to prolong their life. If properly conditioned, violets and pansies will last for almost a week. Blooms should be submerged in cool water for two hours—or preferably, overnight. After this treatment a damp washcloth, or piece of moist cotton, placed over the flowers at night will usually suffice to keep them fresh. However, a bunch of violets, apparently wilted beyond all hope of redemption, can often be revived if submerged in lukewarm water overnight. The same thing applies to hydrangea heads, as well as to pansies and other blooms with similar drinking habits. Pansy garlands which have been wrapped in damp newspaper overnight will hold up for a surprisingly long time without any water at all.

PLATE 9.

The simple vertical placement of five flowers shown in Plate 9 will prove as versatile as arrangements using only three blossoms. The working plan is very easy to follow, and the design lends itself to many types of containers and flowers. Although the arrangement is highly stylized, the natural growth habits of the flowers have not been violated. Stems are grouped around a central axis and the upright flowers reach toward the light just as they would if growing in the garden.

The large round container has particularly beautiful lines. It was made from a harrow and had led a hard life in Louisiana cane fields before a touch of solder and a coat of white paint started it on a new career. The graceful sweep of the curve, which has remained virtually unchanged since its inception many decades ago, proves that utility and beauty go hand in hand. However, not until the disc was introduced to the delicate antique Chinese stand did it really come into its own. Purity of form makes the harrow appear particularly graceful with the slender-legged stand. The combination calls for the most elegant flowers and setting.

PLATE 9 ▶

The rough-textured dark rocks used to cover the needlepoint holder in this design tie in with the coloring of the stand and repeat the texture of the flowers. Their bulk adds necessary weight, as well as giving dignity and elegance to the composition as a whole.

Although it is simpler to create a pleasing design with flowers in varying stages of development, it is an easy matter to compensate for identical blooms by controlled spacing between the flowers. The larger the space between the flower heads the smaller the flower will appear to be. Blossoms placed farther apart at the top of an arrangement than at the base of design will give the illusion of an increase in the size of the blooms. As voids are decreased and flowers placed more compactly together the blooms themselves appear larger.

There was very little variety in the sizes of the chrysanthemums used in Plate 9; therefore, the flower with the longest and most pleasing stem was selected for the central placement. The stem was kept at maximum length in view of the vertical design and the visual weight of the container. Even in small containers, a vertical design where blossoms are held close to the main line can be quite tall without appearing top-heavy.

1. Place chrysanthemum #1 in the center of the needlepoint holder as indicated on diagram C (Drawing III). The tip of the flower should be immediately over the base of the stem, and each succeeding bloom stem should be impaled as close as possible to the original placement.

2. Cut blossom #2 seven inches shorter than #1 and place it to the left of, and slightly behind, the first blossom. The head of the flower should be quite close to the first stem.

3. Cut stem #3 five inches shorter than #2 and impale on the holder to the right and slightly in front of #1. The head of this bloom should swing a little farther away from the first placement than #2.

4. Cut stem #4 three inches shorter than #3 and impale as close as possible to #1 and #2, with the bloom head leaning slightly toward the left front of the container.

5. The last chrysanthemum should be cut two inches shorter than #4. It should be impaled as close as possible to #3 and #4 with the blossom tilted toward the right front of the container, between points 4 and 5 on diagram C.

6. Cover the unused portion of needles with glass slag, moss, or some other suitable material. Care should be exercised to mantain vertical feeling of design and to avoid a piled-up effect.

7. A final check should show all flowers reaching up toward the light, all stems apparently emanating from the same central growth, and no two flowers the same distance from each other. The blooms should flow in measured rhythm, carrying the eye smoothly through the design without monotony or jerkiness.

SUMMARY

1. Both approaches given in this chapter for using "three plus two" are capable of infinite expansion. Many variations are possible.

2. The illusion of a garden scene may be created by two correctly proportioned branches; the most pleasing effects are obtained by simulating natural habits of growth.

3. Any low-growing flower that looks well under a tree will look well framed by two properly scaled branches; best results are obtained by featuring the "tree," *not* the blossoms growing at its feet.

4. Bare branches usually require less visual weight at the base of the design than compositions incorporating flowering shrubs.

5. A small container will balance a very tall arrangement if all flower heads are kept within the periphery of container.

6. Flowers that normally have tall, straight stems are ideal for vertical five-flower arrangements.

7. Five flowers of the same color and variety, in different stages of development, are simplest to arrange.

8. Regardless of variation in size of blossoms, voids *between* blooms should vary with each placement.

9. The blooms *and voids* should flow through the design, drawing the eye smoothly from the tip to the base of the arrangement.

10. With the proper container, flowers, and stand, a suitable five-point design can be worked out for *any* home.

THREE

MASS ARRANGEMENTS WITH MINIMUM MATERIAL

CONTRARY TO COMMON OPINION, NATURE GIVES AS MANY POINTERS FOR MAKING MASS ARRANGEMENTS AS FOR LINE or "naturalistic" designs.

A study of the methods employed by nature in massing wild flowers will prove most helpful. They seldom grow in sharply defined areas; each variety trails gracefully out into the other. Pleasing drifts draw the eye so effortlessly through transitions that it is often difficult to distinguish where one form starts and the other ends.

PLATE 10.

The three groups of flowers in Plate 10 are related through color and texture; they follow a logical sequence of forms which reaches a natural climax in the asters at the center of the arrangement. Careful relationship of size, shape, texture, and color creates a oneness that makes a small bunch of gypsophila, a half-dozen stock, and a few asters as effective as several dozen flowers.

◄ PLATE 10

If the shape of available plant material is carefully considered and a suitable pattern decided upon, mass arrangements will fall easily into place. The basic design principles are identical, whether you are working with three flowers or three dozen. It is merely a matter of visualizing the shapes of the flowers and leaves and predicting with accuracy the part these forms will play in the chosen design.

Roughly speaking, plants fall into three basic groups: spike forms (larkspur, delphinium, stock); rounded forms, (roses, dahlias, asters); and small composite or indefinite forms, (gypsophila, caspia, phlox). Each group is particularly suited to a specific function in flower arranging. Spike, or tapering, forms tend to fade into the background; placed on the outside edges of a design they flow smoothly into the arrangement. Small or indefinite forms are logical fillers; they give body to the arrangement, releasing attention and directing it toward the center of interest. Bold or rounded forms demand attention, effortlessly holding interest at point of greatest emphasis.

With careful handling *any* form may be made to lead, direct, or hold the eye. However, pleasing designs are more *easily* made when material is allowed to play the part its form suggests—small or indefinite forms releasing attention, bold forms arresting or holding attention. It is as simple as that!

The stock in Plate 10 creates an interesting silhouette and carries the eye easily into the heart of the design. The gypsophila, thickening toward the center of the arrangements, fills in voids and provides necessary transition between the stock and asters; it strews beauty along the way, but the bold form of the asters effortlessly holds the center of the stage. Although the base of the design gives a feeling of solidarity, the flowers are far enough apart to breathe freely. A good way to avoid an unpleasant packed effect at the center of mass arrangements is to follow the Oriental example and "leave room for the butterflies to go through."

The placement plan for the mass arrangement shown in Plate 10 is identical with plan used in Plate 1, except for the fact that three *groups* of flowers instead of three individual blooms are involved. The three placements of pink stock, which introduce the eye to the design, were cut and placed according to the directions given for the three irises in Plate 1, except that the stems were impaled on outside needles to allow for working space at the center of the design. The gypsophila, strengthening the body of the arrangement and directing attention toward the center of interest, follows the same general proportions and placement. Even asters forming a center of interest repeat the trilogy.

The inexpensive glass container shown in Plate 10 has little character

44

in itself. However, it gains elegance through the use of a handsome teakwood stand. And again, as in preceding designs, mechanics have been concealed in a manner that adds distinction to the composition. The pink-flecked silica fragments concealing the needlepoint holder not only give necessary weight at the base of the design, but repeat the texture of the glass container and blend with the coloring of the plant material and the base. The close relationship mates all elements together, making even the container seem a living part of the over-all design.

1. Select the three stock with the most interesting tips for the three main placements.

2. Referring to Plate 10 and diagram A (Drawing IV), cut stock #1 to desired tallest length. The height of the central placement should be suited not only to the container, but to the location and use for which the arrangement is intended.

3. Shorten the other two stems proportionately, bearing in mind both location and purpose.

4. Impale stock #1 at center of holder, in the position indicated on diagram A (Drawing IV). The most pleasing side of the flower stalk should face you, and the tip of the bloom should fall immediately over the base of the stem.

5. Select stock #2 with a tip which can be made to curve slightly upward. Place the stock in an upright position at the far left edge of the holder. Press down firmly on the inside lower end of the stem, forcing the blossom to the desired angle (about 30 degrees). The bloom should follow line 7 on diagram A, and the tip should curve up toward first placement.

6. Impale stock #3 on the front right edge of the holder in an upright position. Press down on the side of the stem until the blossom remains where you want it (at about a 45-degree angle). The bloom should reach out toward you between points 3 and 4 on diagram A, and the tip should curve up toward the first placement.

7. Strengthen #1, #2, and #3 with remaining stock. The additional stems should be close to the original placements, but the blooms should not overlap.

8. Group gypsophila into about a dozen fairly compact bunches. Green thread is preferable for holding the small stems together; however, twine, tape, elastic bands, or any available device may be used.

9. Cut the gypsophila for center placement several inches shorter than stock #1. Shorten the other two groups of gypsophila proportionately.

10. Strengthen #1, #2, and #3 with gypsophila. The gypsophila should

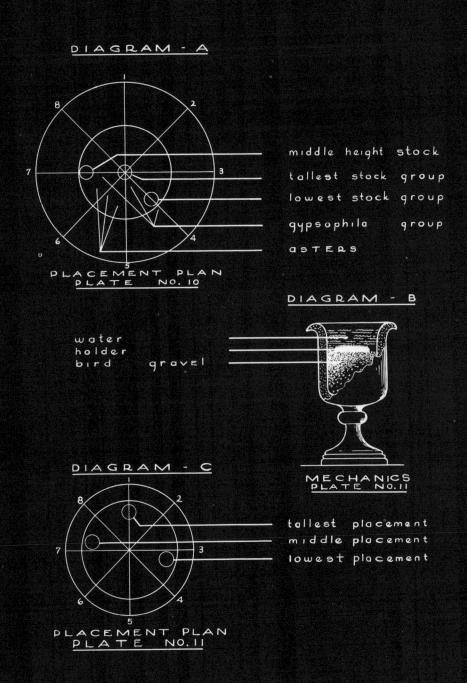

DIAGRAM - A

middle height stock

tallest stock group

lowest stock group

gypsophila group

asters

PLACEMENT PLAN
PLATE NO. 10

water
holder
bird gravel

DIAGRAM - B

MECHANICS
PLATE NO. 11

DIAGRAM - C

tallest placement

middle placement

lowest placement

PLACEMENT PLAN
PLATE NO. 11

Drawing IV, with diagrams for Plates 10 and 11.

trail gracefully up into the stock and become more compact toward the center of the design.

11. Add the asters, following the line direction of stock #1 and checking to be sure that the asters balance the design.

12. Cover the unused portion of needles with silica, glass slag, or some other suitable material. Carefully placed aster foliage might serve this purpose; however, too many added leaves at the base of the design will look unnatural and may be worse than a few needles showing.

PLATE 11.

Mass arrangements often contain a distinct design within the over-all pattern, such as that formed by the roses and carnations in Plate 11. The boundaries, or silhouette, of the arrangement may be triangular, oval, circular, etc.; while the heart of the design, or center of interest, instead of repeating this outline, forms a graceful curve or lazy S.

The S, or reverse, curve was known to Greek artists and architects as the beauty line, or line of beauty. William Hogarth (1697-1764), English painter, engraver, and satirist, stressed the point to such an extent that this graceful line is now known as the Hogarth curve. Oriental arrangers are very conscious of this beauty line, and with a little imagination it may be discerned in any Japanese design. Faulty arrangements can often be improved by adjusting material so that the eye follows such a curve.

The large, elaborate design in Plate 11 is suited to the formality of a Georgian or Colonial drawing room. The arrangement contains only three gladioli, two stock, and two carnations, combined with spirea, three roses, five Dutch irises, and a single hyacinth from the garden.

Full advantage was taken of the long, graceful spirea by removing the leaves and using the sprays to form the outer edges of the design. In this way interesting voids, as well as the lacy blooms, lead the eye into the arrangement.

Expert handling of voids is essential in creating mass arrangements with a minimum amount of material. The shape and location of voids, or spaces between flowers, plays as important a part in the design as the plant material itself. Large voids and very little plant material should constitute the outer edges of the arrangement, with more material and smaller voids developing toward the center of design. The gradual decrease in the size of the voids should continue until the heart of the arrangement appears to be a solid "mass" of flowers. Flowers should not overlap or appear packed, but no voids should be visible at the center of a well-constructed mass arrangement.

The tips of the glads and stock in Plate 11 flow naturally out into the spirea, drawing the eye into the denser part of the design. Open florets of these spike forms strengthen the body of the arrangement, directing attention toward the center of interest. Although the photograph shows a sharp contrast between dark roses and light carnations, they did not actually vie for attention. The dubonnet roses and dusty pink carnations made a pleasing flow of color at the center of the otherwise white design.

The alabaster container in Plate 11 reflects coloring and texture of flowers, while the simple, classic shape of the urn gives stability and balance to the design. If the gladioli and stock had been used at outside of the design, with the spirea as a filler, the arrangement would have appeared heavier and a base would have been required to give proper balance. One or more stands similar to those shown in Plate 1 would prove ideal with this formal type of container.

In order to make the most of short-stemmed flowers and simplify control of material in the tall urn, the holder was raised as near the top of the container as practicable. This was done by filling the container two-thirds full of bird gravel and placing a large needlepoint holder on top of the gravel. Bird gravel becomes compact when dampened and will support even the heaviest holder without wobbling. Builders' sand does not give as firm a footing, but it will do the job if nothing better is available. The secret is to dampen, but not saturate, the gravel before starting to work. For best results additional water should not be put into container until the arrangement has been placed in the location for which it is intended.

If greater stability is desired the holder may actually be sealed into the container. A half-inch of paraffin or melted candle wax on top of the dry gravel will do the trick. The wax should be just warm enough to pour without lumping, and the holder should be seated in the wax immediately. The wax should set for at least two hours or, preferably, overnight. This will assure a waterproof seal, and the holder will then remain in place permanently or until heat is applied to melt wax.

1. Fill the container one-half to two-thirds full of bird gravel or any substance firm enough to support a large needlepoint holder.

2. Place the holder on top of the dampened gravel, keeping the tips of the needles two or three inches below the lip of the container in

PLATE 11 ►

order to allow sufficient room for water, as indicated on diagram B (Drawing IV).

3. Create the desired silhouette with spirea as shown on diagram C (Drawing IV). Make the first placement at center-back of the holder; the second placement on the left back edge of the holder, between 7 and 8; and the third placement on the front right edge of the holder, between 3 and 4.

4. Strengthen the center and right-hand placements of spirea with glads, keeping the stems of the glads as close as possible to the original groupings of spirea.

5. Strengthen the left-hand placement of spirea with stock and iris, placing the lower iris blooms closer together than the top ones.

6. Secure the smallest rose on the holder so that the bloom is in line with the center placement of spirea and gladiolus.

7. Group the remaining roses and carnations in a pleasing curve; they should give a feeling of unity, strengthening the main line and balancing the design.

8. Check to be sure that voids, as well as flower forms, flow smoothly into each other.

PLATE 12.

Some plant material, such as stock, snapdragons, gladioli, etc., is made up of two distinct forms and thus may serve a dual purpose. The tips, or buds, may be used to lead the eye into or out of the design, while open florets act as fillers or, in some instances, even form the center of interest. The gladioli in Plate 12 play such a double role. It not only creates the silhouette, but forms the body of the design.

The large vertical arrangement is composed of only two white glads, two stock, two white caladium leaves, and three callas. The tip of the arrangement carries the eye upward even beyond the actual design, thus adding to the mystic feeling created by the simple vertical thrust of the gladioli.

The calla lilies and caladium leaves, forming the center of interest, have been grouped so as to give a more or less circular effect. This treatment allows the tips of the lilies and caladium leaves to flow into the gladioli, thus concentrating attention at the point of greatest emphasis.

PLATE 12 ►

The heart-shaped caladium leaves lead the eye into the arrangement and start it traveling upward through the gladioli. The tall, cylindrical container lends itself admirably to the simple aspirational design. The circular stands, repeating the form of the gray pottery container, give unity to the composition and add necessary weight at the base of the visually heavy design.

Before starting on the vertical arrangement in Plate 12, the holder was lifted as near to the top of the cylindrical container as practicable, using the method explained in the description of Plate 11. The design was then created in the same manner as the triangular arrangement shown in Plate 11. The silhouette was established first, working the glads from the center-back and right side of the holder, and using stock for the left-hand placement. Lilies were then added and the two caladium leaves placed for greater emphasis. Although the center of the arrangement has a circular movement, each new placement was carefully checked to be sure it added to, rather than detracted from, the vertical thrust of the over-all design.

SUMMARY

1. Mass arrangements are more easily constructed if three different plant forms are incorporated into the design.
2. Study the shape of the plant material and analyze the part each form is to play in a chosen design.
3. The use of more than five varieties in one arrangement is apt to create confusion unless very skillfully handled.
4. A needlepoint holder near the top of a tall container will give better control of material than chicken wire or similar devices.
5. Repetition of texture, form, or color in plant material and container helps achieve necessary unity.
6. Working from the outside of the holder toward the center of the design eliminates unsightly needles at the sides and gives necessary working space at the center of the arrangement.
7. Height and width should be established with the first three placements, and nothing should extend beyond this silhouette.
8. Boundaries of the design should merge into the background, with voids gradually decreasing and solids increasing toward the center of the arrangement.
9. The more voids and the less plant material at the outer edges of the design, the larger the arrangement can be without appearing top-heavy.
10. Repetition with calculated change should carry the eye smoothly through transitions of size, shape, texture, and color.

FOUR

MAKING COLOR WORK FOR YOU

IT DOES NOT TAKE AN ELECTRICAL ENGINEER TO USE ELEC-
TRICITY INTELLIGENTLY. NOR DOES EFFECTIVE HANDLING OF
color depend upon a master's degree in art. It is simply a matter of
knowing which switch to flick and where it is located.

The fine points governing the working mechanism of the switch and
its relationship to a hydroelectric plant are tremendously interesting,
but they involve years of intensive study. Knowing what creates specific
colors in flowers and how to reproduce these colors with man-made pigments is equally fascinating and does not involve nearly as much study.
However, flower colors, like electricity, come to us ready for use, so
this knowledge is by no means essential to the pleasing arrangement of
flowers.

It is necessary to know only what effect these ready-mixed colors
have on each other and on the observer. A good color wheel will help
locate the proper switch for specific color effects, and practice will teach
us how to operate the switch. (See color wheel, page 61.)

PLATE 13.

Color brings double pleasure when it is skillfully planned to set the
desired mood. The green arrangement shown in Plate 13 was designed
to create an impression of coolness on a hot summer day. The glossy,

cool-looking rubber leaves contrast pleasantly with the soft brown palm sheath and old stump which complete the simple five-point arrangement.

The irregular oval shape, as well as the easy-to-blend coloring of the Frankhoma pottery container make it one of the most versatile on the market. Neither lack of storage space nor a limited budget need confine the arranger to a few types of flowers or designs. A large collection of containers is definitely *not* necessary. With a container of the kind shown in Plate 13, and one the shape of the container in the following plate, *any* flower and *any* design may be satisfactorily worked out.

The green pottery container with its brown overglaze repeats the coloring and texture of both sheath and leaves. The new growth springing from the old stump and the irregular outline of the brown plaque beneath the arrangement add to the naturalistic poolside effect. The deep shadows, as well as the harmony of form, give a feeling of restful coolness even in the black-and-white photograph. Setting a mood through the *illusion* of color is an excellent test, for color is only one element of our art and should always be secondary to design.

A good flower arrangement, like a well-designed garden, is pleasing even when stripped of color.

PLATE 14.

Golden daffodils and forsythia were combined in Plate 14 to brighten a dark room and create the illusion of warmth on a cold, wintry day. Very little basic knowledge is required in order to know which colors will lighten a dark corner, make a small room give the illusion of space, foreshorten a large room, warm up a cold-looking one, or create a feeling of coolness on a hot summer day. We have only to study the colors nature has placed all around us.

Bright orange, yellow, and red gaillardia flaming across the prairie, poppies flowing like liquid sunshine over far hills, seem to come forward to greet us—they demand attention. These are the warm, glowing colors, reminding us of sunshine and of heat. Wild violets nestling shyly beneath cool, dark leaves, blue swamp iris hiding on the shadowy water's edge, their colors blending with the atmosphere—these create a feeling of coolness and of space.

Nature's simple logic makes mood-setting colors very easy to remember. The sun colors—orange, red, and yellow—the colors of fire—are the warm, or advancing, colors. The blues, greens, and violets of distant horizons—the colors of water and of ice—are the cool, receding colors.

The sunshine colors in Plate 14, as well as the texture of the flowers, are repeated in the simple yellow pillow vase with brown overglaze. The dark brown base and lighter brown driftwood also pick up the coloring and texture of flowers and stems, which are repeated again in the golden-brown fungi used to complete the design. This blending of earth colors with the color of sunshine is one that is frequently employed by nature. When you are in doubt about a color scheme, individual flowers will often supply the answer. The many varieties of brown and yellow flowers prove this combination to be a particularly happy one.

A study of nature's favorite color schemes will prove as rewarding as the all-important study of her design principles. The most inept colorist will achieve pleasing results by concentrating on nature's favorite combinations. Even the difficult-to-blend blue-reds and orange-reds will prove satisfactory if we do as nature does in her landscapes and add generous quantities of blue or green. Almost any flower will look well in a gray-green (grass) or soft brown (earthy) container. Sky blue, also, will prove surprisingly versatile.

Vivid containers are apt to detract from the subtle coloring of flowers, they will be much more satisfactory if they are toned down. If a too bright, or too shiny, container is dipped in buttermilk, it will acquire a soft patina, which is easy to work with. Tempera, water colors, or shoe polish may also be used, but buttermilk washes off more easily.

Pillow vases are copied from the block used as a pillow by the Japanese and are very easy to work with. The simple lines are a satisfactory foil for a diversity of designs and flowers. However, containers should repeat some color, or feeling of color, in the plant material, so the bright yellow container in Plate 14 would have only limited use without the brown overglaze. The earthiness of the brown tones it down and makes it suitable for many different types of flowers.

As in previous designs (Plates 11 and 12), the holder in Plate 14 was lifted near the top of container to simplify control of the material. The silhouette was then formed by making the first placement at center-back of the holder. The forsythia stems were placed as close together as possible, with the blooms forming a graceful curve. Driftwood was then added to cover bare stems and to give necessary weight at the base of the composition. The driftwood forming the upper part of the design was soaked in hot water to make it soft enough to impale on the needlepoint holder. The lower piece of wood was wired to two small forsythia stems, as outlined in diagram A (Drawing V). The stems were then

PLATE 14

PLATE 15

impaled on the holder so that the wood could hang down and curve over the lip of the container.

The smallest daffodil, facing the left side of the container, was cut shorter than the top piece of wood and placed immediately behind it. The two succeeding blossoms were each brought a little forward and turned slightly more toward the front of the design, thus giving depth to the arrangement. Spaces between the daffodil blooms were decreased toward the center of the design, and wire was inserted in the stem of the lowest flower as outlined in the discussion of Plate 6. The lower daffodil stem was impaled on the back right-hand needles with the bloom swinging forward and around the main placement. This treatment added to the feeling of depth and completed the main body of the Hogarth curve, which actually terminated in the brown and yellow fungi at the base of the design. A few elæagnus leaves served as transitional material and helped create an effect of new growth springing from the old wood.

PLATE 15.

Living, growing colors may be woven into a pleasing picture without knowing how to describe color accurately. However, it is helpful to know what will prove harmonious. In order to identify the "tunes," some knowledge of the three qualities of color is essential. A study of the arrangement shown in Plate 15 will reveal a number of the principles involved in the harmonious blending of color.

Each color or hue has a family of its own—three sepaarte groups of colors with the same blood line. The groups are as distinct as the three shapes, or forms, of plant material—and, with a little study, they will prove as easy to identify. A color that has been lightened by the addition of white becomes a *tint*—another *value*—of the original hue. Red even changes its name to pink! Red darkened with black becomes dubonnet— a *shade*, another *value* of the original color; while red toned down by gray (equal parts of black and white) becomes dusty rose, another *tone* of red. Accurate identification of these three color forms will eliminate much misunderstanding.

Countless excellent books have been written on the subject of color, any one of which will prove helpful. However, the *Handbook for Flower Shows*, put out by National Council of Garden Clubs, Inc., gives an excellent condensation. An hour's study, starting at page 91 of the handbook, should enable the rank amateur to identify and describe color accurately by:

1. *HUE:* Quality and character of a specific color—the *name* of the color. (Is it yellow or orange?)
2. *VALUE:* Degree of lightness or darkness, the amount of black *or* white it contains. (Is it a tint or a shade?)
3. *CHROMA:* Intensity—the brightness of the *tone*, or the dullness. (Is it a pure color, or a grayed tone?)

The two celadon containers in Plate 15 were first lifted to different levels, and then placed close together on one large base with the plant material forming a single design. The neighboring tints, tones, and shades of violet, blue, and red flow from lightness to darkness. The lighter tints form the outside edges of the arrangement, with the deeper tones and shades appearing toward the center of the design.

On the left, pale pink stock works down into deeper pink stock and still darker snapdragons, reaching a climax in the deep red roses. The pale lavender caspia and very pale blue vitex on the right of the design take on deeper tones near the center, blending with bright blue agapanthus, deep lavender asters, and purple grapes at the base of the design.

This flowing from light to dark is the easiest possible way to handle color. When spike material is also the lightest color (the one containing the largest quantity of white), both form *and* color fade into the background and help lead the eye into the arrangement. The deepening of color as the plant material becomes more compact toward center of arrangement helps balance the design and direct attention toward the point of emphasis.

It is much more difficult to reverse the process and balance dark or brilliant spike material at the outside edges of the design with lighter material at the center. This procedure requires careful handling, since the more attention a color attracts the more it seems to weigh, and the larger the area the lighter it appears to be. A very large area of light color is needed at the base of the design to balance dark or brilliant color at the outer edges. When colors flow naturally from light to dark, the center of the design can be as small as the darkness or brilliance of the material warrants, thus lessening the danger of poorly proportioned color values. The Greeks probably took their famous design formula from nature, for she frequently uses three parts light color and two parts secondary color to balance a very small area of brilliant color.

The bright red roses forming center of interest or focal point in Plate 15 emphasize the subtle values of other plant material, and the contrast of color gives character to the design even when it is viewed from a distance. Blues and lavenders blend with the atmosphere and are apt to lose their identity unless seen close up under ideal lighting conditions. Reflected light has such a drastic effect on color that it is best to try

COLOR WHEEL

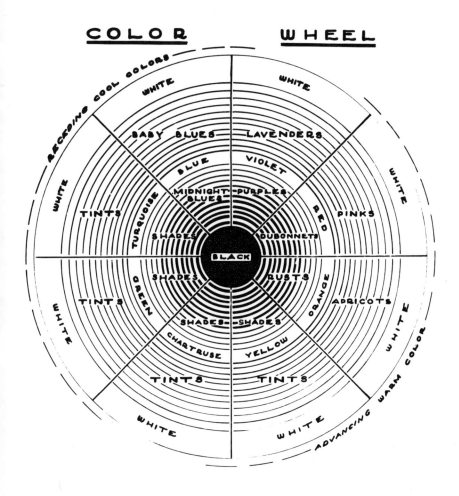

Color Wheel. Many spike flowers grow in closely related (analogous) colors, with small dark buds at the tip of the stalk balanced by lighter colored large open florets at the base (delphinium, larkspur, gladioli, etc.). Rounded forms frequently show maximum contrast (complementary colors): red poinsettias with chartreuse centers, purple pansies with yellow throats, blue anemone with an orange eye, etc. Holding gray triple-sheer in front of a bright red poinsettia will give a graphic picture of the way colors are weakened or dulled (toned down) by the addition of gray.

out new colors before incorporating them into a design. If used where lighting has a yellowish cast, lavenders and blues will prove very disappointing, even at close range. The yellow kills the soft color, making the flowers appear dull and muddy.

Flowers are not composed of static pigments; there is a constant chemical change. It is wise, therefore, to find out how time will affect the material before incorporating it into a color scheme. Some of the changes are not immediately visible to the naked eye, but we have all seen red roses acquire a definitely bluish cast after a day or two in the house. Since the flow of color in Plate 15 was built around blues and violets, the roses would remain effective regardless of this change.

SUMMARY

1. Nature's handling of color problems is an essential study for the flower arranger.

2. A color wheel will prove helpful, even though flower colors come to us ready mixed.

3. *Any* color can be used effectively with any other color by following the example nature sets and incorporating generous quantities of blue or green.

4. When looking for versatile containers, you will find that the gray-blue of the sky, the soft browns of the earth, or the gray-green of the grass will often prove more effective than the neutrals—pure gray, black, or white.

5. Pleasing results are more easily achieved if the heavier or most brilliant colors are placed at the base of the design and the lighter colors at the outer edges.

6. Colors should flow smoothly through the arrangement, holding the eye effortlessly at the point of greatest emphasis.

7. The stimulating colors that carry well from a distance are the fire and sun colors—red, orange, and yellow. The restful, receding colors that must be at close range to be fully enjoyed are the cool violets, blues, and greens of water and ice.

8. The visual weight of color is based on the attention it attracts. Three parts light color and two parts secondary color will balance a very small area of brilliant color at the center of the design.

9. It takes a very large area of light or dull color at center of design to balance a small area of dark or brilliant color on bounding edges.

10. The most pleasing designs usually feature either *very closely related colors* or *maximum contrast*.

FIVE

THE FOUR SIDES OF YOUR TABLE

THE SIMPLEST WAY TO MAKE TABLES INTERESTING FROM ALL SIDES, AS WELL AS TO ACHIEVE DRAMA WITH MINIMUM material and expense, is to feature a piece of sculpture.

The two-foot bronze monkey in Plate 16, combined with four leaves from a house plant, was the topic of conversation at a large political reception. Even a two-*inch* figurine, with correctly proportioned foliage, would prove equally as effective if it were scaled to the table and to the room in which it was used. The decorative motif should be in proportion to the table and the other things on the table, as well as related through color and texture to the room and its furnishings.

An eighteen-foot table—and no funds—posed quite a problem until "Ao" and the *Monstera deliciosa* leaves took over. The beauty of the dark bronze monkey and exotic deep green leaves was emphasized through the use of a glossy black base and a floor-length red burlap tablecloth. A brass samovar on one end of the table and a large inlaid brass tray and punch bowl on the other completed the picture.

Ample space was left on the table for sandwich trays and other serving pieces large enough to take care of the expected crowd. Table setting, like flower arranging, is a matter of good taste and common sense. While there is no hard and fast rule governing any art, there is one absolute must to setting a table. Functionability comes first—a table *must* be suited to the purpose for which it is intended. Table-setting conventions are the outgrowth of custom—guides for gracious living based on this factor. Cloths centered and hanging twelve to sixteen inches from floor (lace longer, but *not* long enough for people to trip over); candle flames above or below eye level of guests; even the accepted placement of flat silver, glasses, etc.—all these customs were worked out to promote ease and convenience.

The comfort of family and friends is considered in grouping furniture and placing lamps, yet many an otherwise considerate hostess designs centerpieces that cling tenaciously to goblet stems or droop petals into the whipped cream or butter. Although the decorative motif is of prime importance, it should *never* interfere with the ease of service.

Many things that are feasible in one generation are, through changed living conditions, outmoded in the next. However, the gracious serving of food has for centuries remained a gauge of good taste and breeding. Since our daily lives reflect the times in which we live there is no limit to the innovations we may make, but the changes should be functional as well as beautiful. Today's trend is toward streamlining, and many tables (as well as flower arrangements) are spoiled by overcrowding. Here—as in all other arts—there is great strength in simplicity.

PLATE 16.

Complete simplicity, as well as close relationship with the room, added to the dramatic effect of the table shown in Plate 16. The texture of the cloth repeated the texture of the walls, and the color of the burlap tied in with the highly polished brick floor. The shiny black base also picked up the sheen of waxed floor, and the dark bronze monkey repeated the color and texture of the brown leather chairs. The repetition of texture made feasible a strong contrast of color, just as restatement of color is often enhanced by a contrast in textural qualities. The cloth supplied not only brilliant color, but also the only rough texture in the composition. The black, shiny base, placed directly on the coarse cloth, gave maximum contrast of texture and color. Although everything else on the table repeated the darkness, as well as the sheen, of the base, none of the other elements were quite as dark or quite as glossy.

The high-ceilinged room had neither curtains nor pictures; it con-

PLATE 16 ►

tained only the heavy table and twelve equally large, dark brown leather chairs. The polished brick floor, the painted brick and natural striated plywood walls, together with the heavy, exposed rafters of the ceiling, called for bold forms and no fussiness. Everything on the table was scaled not only to the table itself, but to the room and its furnishings. The coarse red cloth and oversized black base made a strong but pleasing contrast of both color and texture, dramatizing and giving warmth to the austere room.

The leatherlike base was made by wrapping two asbestos shingles in several layers of newspaper and then covering them with heavy "patent leather" paper. This decorative paper may be obtained at most department stores and comes in many colors and patterns. Whether you are looking for the finest marble, raw silk, top-grain leather, knotty pine, or even a brick wall, the paper manufacturers have anticipated your wants! With a little imagination and careful handling of folds around the corners, this type of paper will solve many problems.

The size of the reception table and the lack of funds were prime factors, so the first step was to think of an inexpensive way to cover the required space. The decorative motif should occupy between one sixth and one third of the table length, which meant an arrangement between three and five feet long. The two eighteen-inch square shingles gave necessary length and width, while the monkey supplied height and visual weight to the large design. A simple bronze container placed on two blocks of polished wood served as a foundation for the driftwood "tree." The monkey was placed as close as possible to the container, and the two bronzes were treated as a single unit. The *Monstera* seemed to be growing on the "tree"; two leaves followed the graceful curve of the monkey's head and shoulders, while a single leaf arched across his back, repeating the curve on the other side of the design. Dried South African figs and bronze giant wandering Jew added weight and solidarity to the base of the picture.

When the arrangement was completed, "Ao" seemed to be actually leaning against the container intently studying the small, rock-covered "pool" at the foot of the "tree." The monkey in his tropical setting, gazing pensively at a jade frog perched on the edge of the bronze container, tells a story that would prove interesting even without the hard-to-come-by *Monstera* fruit which was used for the center of interest.

The frog on the side of the pool was an afterthought and gave just the right finishing touch for those who took time to examine the arrangement closely. Small details of this kind may be added to a completed design, but larger objects should be a part of the over-all pattern, and must therefore be placed before the design is started.

In featuring a piece of sculpture, or using an accessory, it is more interesting to have the figure tell a story. Therefore, one that expresses action, either actual or implied, is usually more stimulating than a head or some other static carving.

For this reason, the ebony head in Plates 17 and 18 proved a bit more difficult than the monkey in preceding plate. The front view of the table shows "Mango" gazing wistfully out over "waves" of ti leaves, while the rear view depicts the lush tropical fruits of her native island.

The arrangement was planned for a farewell dinner at a club. The large oval table seated twenty-four guests; it was placed in front of a mirrored wall, and both sides of the centerpiece were visible to the guests when they entered the room.

Purchasing a tablecloth for the oval table was not feasible, but the arrangement would have lost much of its charm had it been placed directly on the club's plain white cloth. Two yards of chartreuse raw silk provided a runner which gave the necessary area of color and tied the decorative motif in with the formal, elegant room. A runner of this kind will prove as versatile as a good stand and can be used over and over again. Out-of-the-home tables that are difficult to decorate can be inexpensively and effectively tied into the decor of the room by the simple device of a well-chosen strip of cloth. Those who are often called upon to decorate for large affairs will find a supply of runners an excellent investment.

The runner in Plates 17 and 18 picked up the texture, as well as the touch of chartreuse, of the predominantly coral chairs surrounding the table and of the room's sixteen elaborately draped windows. The chartreuse raw silk also served to unify the large design by repeating the coloring of the chrysanthemums as well as of the fruits and vegetables forming the back of the arrangement.

Again, as in the preceding plate, a paper-wrapped shingle supplied the base for an oversized design, and again black patent-leather paper proved the perfect complement for the piece of sculpture. A small box, wrapped in the same paper, was placed beneath the head to give it additional height. Only one shingle was used, so placed that the points introduced the eye to the design from both ends and sides of the table. The fruit trailed off the back point, while the front point followed the direction of the runner and disappeared under the heavy green leaves, as indicated in diagram B (Drawing V).

Ti leaves are an excellent buy. They are available the year round, stay green for weeks, and dry beautifully. The leaves purchased for

PLATE 17

PLATE 18

table depicted in Plates 17 and 18 were no exception. They were used in varying stages of greenness and finally appeared as Christmas decorations. They are shown in "September Morn," Plate 25; with the sleepy lion in Plate 26; again as a foil for "Mango," but in their dried state, in Plate 27; and finally with Christmas balls as the center of interest in Plate 28.

Before starting the design in Plates 17 and 18, the runner, base, and head were placed on the table and studied from the main doorway. Both the front and mirror views were considered in order to determine the most dramatic angle for guests entering the room. Since a container would have interrupted the flow of the design, a coffee can, which could be easily concealed, was used to hold water. The can, with a large needlepoint holder in it, was placed as close as possible to the head, and another holder was placed immediately behind the can to take care of the fruit and vegetables, which did not require water.

The proper height and width were first established with ti leaves. The lower leaves were curled to represent rolling waves; the top ones were arranged to look as much as possible like a banana tree. The chrysanthemums were then placed in a graceful Hogarth curve, with buds forming the top and bottom of the design. The corresponding curve on the reverse side of the design was formed with cucumber water lilies (see diagram C, Drawing V), avocados, green peppers, and grapes with variegated philodendron trailing through them. Since the philodendron required water, it shared the coffee can with the ti leaves and chrysanthemums.

Although entirely different material was used to create a completely different feeling, the two sides of the arrangement were so well integrated that unity was apparent regardless of the angle from which the design was viewed. The centerpiece not only tied in with the decor of the room and told a story, but went a step further and told an appropriate story! The guests of honor were about to embark on a cruise to the South Sea Islands. "Mango," extending a welcoming hand across the breaking waves of ti leaves, represented the mystery of the islands with exotic, lush fruits forming a rhythmic pattern in the background.

PLATE 19.

The concept of beauty remains flexible, and line designs are just as effective in traditional rooms as the usual mass arrangements. It is necessary only for the container and plant material to be in keeping

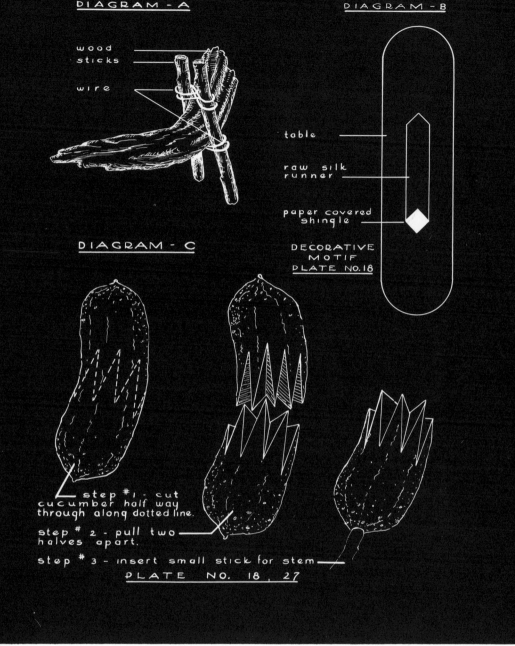

DIAGRAM-A

wood sticks
wire

DIAGRAM - B

table
raw silk runner
paper covered shingle

DECORATIVE MOTIF
PLATE NO.18

DIAGRAM - C

step #1 - cut cucumber half way through along dotted line.

step #2 - pull two halves apart.

step #3 - insert small stick for stem

PLATE NO. 18, 27

Drawing V, with diagrams for Plates 18 and 27.

with the influence of the room and its furnishings. Our heritage from the past, instead of inhibiting, should serve as an inspiration for interpreting the present. Even the most authentic period room leans heavily upon the art and scientific skill of many schools and centuries. By careful blending, the truly beautiful from *any* period — our own included—may be adapted to the beauty from any other era.

Three- and five-point arrangements are interesting from all sides and are, therefore, ideal for tables. If suitable containers were substituted, the designs shown in the first two chapters would make ideal table arrangements. With proper textural relationship, even the very tall arrangements in Plates 7 and 8 would prove satisfactory. The slender branches would not interfere with conversation, so they could be incorporated even into intimate tables seating less than eight people, which ordinarily call for centerpieces not more than twelve or fourteen inches in height.

In this enlightened age there is very little excuse for falling back on the old stand-by pincushion design of roses, or a fan of gladioli. However, with very little imagination, even these overworked patterns can be made almost as stimulating as streamlined contemporary arrangements. It is simply a matter of grouping colors and varying the design within the over-all pattern, which is known today as the center of interest. There is no limit to the variations as long as there is harmony throughout the picture. Guests expecting the customary silver and candlestick treatment will stifle their usual tea-table yawn and hurry to see what is around the corner, if the back and front of the design are subtly different.

A table that is to be viewed from all angles should not be monotonous, it should be pleasing and interesting from all sides. This does not necessarily mean a startling contrast. Texture and coloring of all plant material should remain in keeping with the container and the furnishings of the room. Only enough difference is required to avoid monotony. The usual globular mound of red roses will take on new life from all sides if roses of a different value form a Hogarth curve on one side and a loose bunch of violets, surrounded by self-foliage, is used to dress up the other side. The difference will be discernible from almost any angle, and even the most blasé guest will want to see what the other side of the table looks like.

Plate 19 shows the decorative motif for a dinner table incorporating traditional silver and damask cloth. The sophisticated design complements the Georgian room and its furnishings as well as the cloth, silver, and nineteenth-century china which were used to complete the table. The diagonal line of pink snapdragons and gladioli gives the table an

PLATE 19

air of elegance which would have required several dozen flowers if arranged in the manner usually associated with this type of setting.

The two candelabra were placed on the table first and the arrangement was made around them. The tips of the line go behind one candlestick and in front of the other, making them an integral part of the design and creating an entirely different effect from all four sides of the table. When candles are properly incorporated into the decorative motif they do much to lift a table. However, like any other accessory, they should never be stuck in as an afterthought. They will usually blend into the over-all picture better if they are either the color of the tablecloth or paler than the flowers forming the bounding edge of the arrangement.

The white candles in Plate 19 would have overpowered the arrangement had they been the color of the roses at the center of the design. The white flows smoothly into the over-all composition, whereas dark or brilliant candles would have added disconcerting spots of strong color at the outside edges of the design. It is vital to plan an over-all color scheme for table settings—including candles and other accessories.

The container used in Plate 19 was made by turning the bottom of a vegetable dish (which matched the candelabra) upside down and using it as a base for the top of the dish. A large needlepoint holder was placed as near the back right-hand corner of the container as possible. Stems for the top line of gladioli were started at the back right-hand edge of the holder, and stems for the bottom line on the left outside needles. Each line was worked toward the center of the holder until the stems lacked less than an inch of meeting. The snapdragons were then impaled behind the top line and in front of the bottom line of gladioli. The red roses were grouped in a graceful curve at the point where snaps and glads would have crossed each other had the lines been allowed to meet.

The refined texture and coloring of the flowers carried out the feeling — the elegant *influence* — of the room and tied the modern design in with everything on the table. The ultramodern diagonal line was no more out of place in the traditional room than were the electric lights, air conditioning, ash trays, clothes of the guests, or manner of serving and eating the meal!

Through contrast, the simplicity of the design brought out the true beauty of the period room and its furnishings. A fussy bunch of flowers would have concealed the lovely lines of the container and detracted from, instead of calling attention to, graceful ornamentation on the candelabra.

Candles are by no means limited to traditional settings. The right kind of candles may be incorporated into any table, at any time of day, *provided* the room and table would be improved by the additional light; however, they should always be used in sufficient quantity to be utilitarian.

In flower shows the safest policy is to incorporate candles only into table settings for after-five service, and to protect candles for patio or terrace from the wind, so that the table will meet the all-important requirement of being functional.

SUMMARY

1. The decorative motif should *never* interfere with the ease and convenience of the guests.

2. Tables must be suited to the functions for which they are intended. Buffet or formal tea tables should be set to look best from a standing position. Tables where guests will be seated should be designed from this angle.

3. The decorative motif should be in scale with the table and related through color and texture to the room and its furnishings. Including candles and all accessories, it should occupy between one sixth and one third of the table.

4. For best results, place all the major pieces on the table before starting to work on the decorative motif. Imagine an aerial view of the completed table, visualizing it as guests will first see it, as well as during service of food.

5. Naturalistic three- or five-point arrangements make very effective table designs, regardless of the era of the furnishings.

6. Container and floral material should always reflect the *influence* of the period.

7. Traditional mass arrangements may be pleasingly modernized by grouping colors and varying the center of interest on the back and front of the design.

8. The three elements—the table top, the individual setting or serving pieces, and the decorative motif — should be in scale and related by color and texture.

9. The well-known art principle of "repetition without monotony" is more important in setting a table than in any other art.

10. Outstanding textural relationship will give even a mediocre table distinction. Contrasting textures may be tied together by form or color, just as contrasting colors may often be unified by a repetition of texture.

SIX

WINNING BLUE RIBBONS

THERE ARE MANY THEORIES ABOUT THE DELICATE ART OF
BECOMING A CONSISTENT BLUE RIBBON WINNER. ALL OF
them are worth considering.

Some people contend that top rating hinges upon the use of unusual material; others say unusual treatment of common material is a much surer road to success. The former method definitely has pitfalls, for judges are often imported from different parts of the country and what is considered rare in one section may be common elsewhere.

The giant yucca, curving lechuguilla spikes and delicately blooming prickly pear in Plate 20 are looked upon with awe in some areas and yet are such pests in others that there have been protests against their use in "flower" shows! In some sections even orchids are not on the rare list — they sell for a few cents *a bunch* in Mexico!

Some writers claim blue ribbons hinge on clever ideas; some, on unusual textural relationship. To others superlative coloring is a sure-fire winner, while still others say an outstanding design will do the trick. Many contend that *everything* hinges upon expert workmanship. Undoubtedly *all* of these things help.

Practice in handling your chosen medium is essential in any field. It enables the artist to select and control the material best suited to his purpose. It is as far-fetched to expect top rating in a good flower show without a working knowledge of mechanics as it would be to expect top billing in an opera without years of practice. Those aspiring to blue ribbons must practice and serve an apprenticeship. An isolated ribbon may be won without knowing how to condition or control material; but consistent blue ribbon winners do not guess — they know by experience. Arrangements are judged as they are when the judges see them, *not* as they were when the exhibitor hopefully delivered them to the management.

There is no magic formula, but an intelligent approach will help Regardless of theories, there are three important phases to entering any flower show: a thorough understanding of the schedule, imagination — and practice.

First *study* and *understand* every if, and, and but in the schedule. After the schedule has been thoroughly digested and any doubts cleared up by questioning the chairman of the show, it is time to decide on a specific class. Quality is much more desirable than quantity. One entry, or possibly two entries, will be best; more than three will not prove satisfactory. After the class has been selected, several days should be spent in *imagining* various interpretations. Not until then should material be assembled and *practice* started on experimental designs.

Imagination should have full play, and experimental construction should continue until the idea seems so complete that it is *bound* to be a tricolor. (Getting up in the middle of the night with an idea that can't wait until morning is the acid test. If the family shares your enthusiasm you will probably bring home the ribbon—and even if you don't it will have been worth the effort.)

PLATE 20.

"West of the Pecos" was the result of a class calling for "a composition typifying a specific section of the country," in a show with the over-all theme "These United States."

In an interpretive class such as this, the first questions judges ask are: Does the arrangement comply with the schedule? Does it carry out the theme? Not until these questions are answered do they proceed with an analysis of the fine points of the design and the subtleties of the interpretation.

PLATE 20 ►

WEST OF THE PECOS

The arrangement in Plate 20 is typical of the arid Big Bend Country of Texas, where tender new shoots can survive only in the shelter of a rock ledge, or under the protection of an already established plant. The sparse vegetation, growing in bristling clumps, guards its precious accumulation of moisture with thorns, spikes, stinging nettles, and thick tough skins. Even to those without knowledge of the struggle for survival, the design conveys the interdependence of the closely grouped material.

No container was necessary, since the material did not require water. The angular design was made on a large needlepoint holder placed close to the back corner of the rocklike base. The lower yucca placement, lechuguilla, and prickly pear cling closely to the base, with the yucca giving a feeling of depth to the design by reaching diagonally across the slab. Petrified wood and gnarled, weathered roots cover the mechanics and supply necessary weight at the foot of the upright yucca placement.

The idea for the arrangement came while studying the diversified defense mechanisms evolved through the vegetation's struggle for survival. In lands of little rain, plants must build reserve moisture and defend that priceless cargo against all comers – or die.

Lechuguilla, shown here curving protectively around the delicately blossoming prickly pear, guards its succulent heart from inquisitive nose or hoof by curved, spiked fingers armed with vicious reverse thorns on both sides. The prickly pear has such wicked thorns that cattle seeking its store of life-giving moisture die with perforated intestines and swollen, infected mouths. Although the giant yucca developed height for protection, it still retains a leather-tough skin, needle-sharp tips, and knifelike edges.

Forbidding porcupines of the vegetable kingdom! Some of these strange plants store moisture for two decades, then spend it all on a single magnificent bloom stalk — and shrivel to dust. Beneath the elephantine hide of others, delicate pastel blossoms sleep. After a rain, ethereal flowers spring from their rough, uncompromising sides.

Even had the judges made no award, a deepening interest in the plants around us made the show a worth-while experience for the entire family.

PLATE 21.

The giant yucca in the preceding plate dried a golden brown and became the inspiration, several months later, for the buffet-table class in a city-wide "Christmas Ideas Show."

The broken halo of bronzed yucca, with the tips dipped in gold sparkle for emphasis, formed a background for an unglazed Madonna that had been rubbed with brown shoe polish to a velvetlike sheen. A mayonnaise jar, sprayed with bronze paint, acted as a base for the Madonna and lifted her to the proper height.

Gold Christmas balls repeated the curve of the Madonna's robe, and a homemade brown candle gave stability to the vertical thrust of the yucca. Magenta strawflowers outlined the Madonna and drifted down through the Christmas balls, softening the close analogous color scheme and emphasizing the circular motion of the design. A fragment of petrified wood repeats the magenta of the flowers, picks up the golden browns of the rest of the composition, and adds necessary weight at the base.

The arrangement is shown on a brass tray, and the design of strawflowers and Christmas balls is repeated around a tall brown candle on the other side of the yucca. Each placement of yucca hugged the Madonna closely, forming a crescent on the holder instead of an uninteresting straight line. The curved halo effect achieved by this placement was much more dramatic than the usual flat fan would have been. The concave design framing the Madonna and the convex one forming background for the tall candle on the other side of the yucca gave the composition depth and interest from all sides of the table. Sticks of various lengths impaled on the holder lifted the Christmas balls to different heights; these, together with an extra-large needlepoint holder, were the only mechanical aids. A little of the glitter used on the yucca tips was sprayed on the Christmas balls and on both candles, to help unify the varying elements of the design.

Candles are fun to make and the most fascinating effects can be obtained. The candles in Plate 21 had plaited string for wicks and were made of melted candle ends molded in milk cartons. A half carton of wax was used for the small candle and a full one for the large candle on the reverse side of the design. The soft brown coloring was the result of melting green and red candle ends together, but any color may be obtained by melting the right colored crayons with clear paraffin or white candles. Discarded lipstick ends make wonderful red candles.

Practically anything can be used for molding candles, but pinch bottles or other small-mouthed receptacles have to be broken in release the candles. Ice cream or milk cartons, or similar paper molds, are simplest to use because they are easy to tear off after the wax has hardened.

A funnel makes an ideal Christmas tree candle and running hot

PLATE 21 ►

MADONNA OF THE DESERT

water over the mold will soften the wax sufficiently to release the candle. The trees may be decorated by pouring over them wax that has been whipped with an egg beater, and sprinkling the frothy wax with glitter while it is still soft enough to set.

Real or artificial flowers or foliage dipped in wax may be pinned or molded to candles in many effective designs. Candles decorated with holly make wonderful Christmas presents for those have-everything friends. Lily-of-the-valley candles are ideal for Easter tables. Hatchets and cherries may be incorporated for Washington's Birthday, flags for the Fourth of July — there is no limit to the decorative possibilities!

An important point to remember in candlemaking is that wax is combustible. It does not have to come directly in contact with fire to burst into flame. The safest method is to melt candles or paraffin in a double boiler and pour the liquid off as the wax melts. If the wax in the mold hardens before new liquid is added, the warm wax will soften it sufficiently to give the finished candle a smooth, firm surface.

The primary purpose of the municipal show was to educate the public and develop ingenuity, so the homemade candles and inexpensive Madonna with mayonnaise-jar base used in Plate 21 were an excellent choice. Everything in the arrangement was available to the general public at little or no cost; and the varying values of brown, highlighted with magenta, are colors often encountered in the arid landscape. The appeal of the subtle coloring, as well as the drama achieved with common material, made even the least observant show-goer more conscious of the surrounding beauty.

PLATES 22 AND 23.

The fungus featured in these two compositions would probably be considered exotic regardless of the locale. Born in dank darkness beneath a flooded house, the mushroomlike growth immediately started to twist and turn — seeking sunlight. As the flood receded, lack of water arrested the erratic search for light, and ensuing months of hot dry winds left the unusual toadstools with the consistency and durability of old leather.

This interesting manifestation of nature has lived a varied life since the termite man rescued it from obscurity. The uninformed populace

is still mystified by the sudden popularity of the termite man — as well as by the number of dignified-looking women seen crawling from under houses in the flooded area!

The arrangements in Plates 22 and 23 were inspired by schedules calling for a spring theme and both flower shows were staged in homes. Even though identical themes were interpreted and the same unique fungus was featured in both compositions, two strikingly different moods have been created.

The first flower-show schedule specified "a buffet table to be shown against natural striated plywood walls." Two earthy gnomes on a hand-hewn block of wood (rubbed with brown shoe polish until it matched walls and table of playroom) helped interpret the spring theme in this show. One of the gnomes, shown sleeping beneath the twisted brown fungus, is apparently unaware that bright yellow ranunculuses have burst into bloom above his head. The other elf, hand on chin and head cocked to one side, seems to be debating the problem of awakening his partner to spread the news that spring has come.

A hole bored in the slab of wood held a wide-mouthed medicine jar, which supplied water for the dwarf ranunculuses. A small needle-point holder was placed in the jar and a larger one on the slab of wood immediately behind the jar. Since the mouth of the jar was flush with the slab of wood, concealing mechanics proved a simple problem.

The sleeping gnome was placed in front of the jar with his head resting on a low-growing toadstool, while the wide-awake elf stands in the background on a larger mushroom. The tallest piece of fungus, curving around behind the standing dwarf, gives a circular motion to the design. The other two pieces of fungus follow the same line of direction, but each one swings a little more toward the front of the arrangement. The ranunculuses, starting behind the standing dwarf, form a graceful Hogarth curve that ends in front of the sleeping elf. This treatment gives a great deal of depth to the simple composition and makes it interesting from all sides of the table.

The dark brown fungi and tiny bright yellow ranunculuses with a few green leaves furnish the only smooth surfaces in the otherwise muted brown study of closely related rough textures. The two dwarfs were purchased in different parts of the country; one was bright orange and one was spotted red, green, and yellow. The smooth texture and harsh coloring did not tie in with proposed design, so the old stand-by, brown shoe polish, was applied. When the polish refused to adhere to the shiny surface, the dwarfs were painted with clear shellac and then sprinkled with earth in an effort to get the right color and texture. The particles of soil, clinging to the shellac, subdued their clashing colors and produced a knobby texture that tied in perfectly with the other elements of the design and with the spring theme.

The schedule for design in Plate 23 called for arrangements "interpreting, or complementing," art treasures in the homeowner's extensive gallery. A much more dignified treatment was required in this setting than in the first show. The gallery was done in soft values of brown; and a large bronze figure of Pan, standing on a tawny marble pedestal, posed quite a problem. Surrounded by the browns and tans of last year's cattails, he took on the role of Spring bursting triumphant from a chrysalis of soft brown palm sheaths. As he pipes his spring song pale yellow irises and new chartreuse cattails rise with fresh vigor from the dark brown, exotic fungi at his feet.

Fortunately, the homeowner had no objection to having Pan moved, so he was placed on one side of the pedestal with a tall bronze container at his back. Again, as in Plate 16, the two bronzes were treated as a single unit. One needlepoint holder was placed in the container and another large one on the pedestal immediately in front of the container.

The strong vertical thrust of the cattails repeats the erect feeling of the bronze statue, while the two palm sheaths hug the figure, curving around it and giving depth to the arrangement. The Dutch irises also curve around the figure, framing it and bringing out the varied tones in the bronze statue. Fungi and petrified wood at the base of the design simulate dark swamp growth and emphasize the circular motion set by the round pedestal. The plant material, arranged to look as if Pan were actually rising triumphant from the dark earth, seems to be growing from the bog at his feet.

The design starts naturally with the tawny round pedestal and swings in a graceful Hogarth curve through the fungi, across the feet of Pan, and up through the iris buds, curved tips of palms, and cattails; dropping down the vertical cattail grouping to rest on the open Dutch irises and Pan himself. The soft browns and tans picked up the coloring of the gallery and its furnishings, and the intent of the design was clear, even without the title.

PLATE 24.

"Carioca" was inspired by a class entitled "The Dance," in a show with a musical theme. Lullaby, Love Song, and March Militaire were some of the other classes considered before the idea finally evolved for interpreting both the spirit of the music and the people for which the melody was named.

PLATE 22

SUDDENLY IT IS SPRING

PLATE 23 ►

BIRTH OF SPRING

PLATE 24 ►

CARIOCA

The five brilliant pink blooms and two immature stalks of dubonnet bananas swing from the back of the large container toward the front, repeating the swirling form of the blossoms and fruit.

The vivid coloring and flaring "skirts" of the banana blooms, as well as the rhythm achieved through their placement, are reminiscent of a well-known and universally loved Cariocan. Carmen Miranda with her swirling petticoats and brilliant headdresses was the inspiration for the gay design.

The arrangement was staged in a niche and the importance of shadows cast by overhead lighting was considered in planning the design. Lighting plays such an important part that it is best to clarify this point with the show committee before making an entry. The shadows in "Carioca" not only add to the design, but also serve to further the interpretation by increasing the feeling of savage rhythm and mystery. In addition they help balance the forward thrust of the lowest banana stalk.

In the photograph the bananas on this stalk seem oversized, but this illusion is caused by the fact that they not only reach toward the front of the large arrangement, but that the container was placed diagonally in the niche to help emphasize the feeling of movement. The bananas were in reality the same size as the hand of bananas hiding in the shadows at the center of the design, and only slightly larger than the ones shown on the tallest bloom stalk at the back of the arrangement!

The vivid pink banana blooms and bright dubonnet fruit depicted in Plate 24 would probably be considered exotic anywhere in the United States. Even gardeners in lower Texas and the tropical tip of Florida, where it is possible to grow "red" bananas outdoors, feel they are decidedly choice. The handsome red-ribbed leaves and small compact tree make an interesting picture in the garden before the two-toned blossoms appear. However, the blooms are so tender that conditions must be just right for them to set fruit. The ornate coloring of the blossoms, as well as their smaller size, makes them even more striking in arrangements than the heavier bloom and fruit of ordinary bananas.

The lighter green edges of the glossy container in Plate 24 repeat the coloring and texture of the exotic bloom stalks, while the duller dubonnet bananas blend interestingly with the mahogany stand. The bright, dark green, three-foot pottery container and large dark stand supply the visual weight necessary to balance the vivid blossoms and heavy fruit.

The sleek textures commonly associated with the jungle were emphasized through the use of a rough-textured background. The shiny brass base of the container added just the necessary touch to the ornate gaiety of the design. The arrangement, with its interesting shadows, feeling of motion, and vivid coloring, had an air of sophisticated mystery—a quality associated in our minds not only with the music which the design interpreted, but also with the Cariocans themselves.

Rio—the land of their birth—gay sophisticate of the jungles! Swirling skirts of sultry dancers, jewel-like harbor, mystery of encroaching jungle —all are embodied in the gay design.

SUMMARY

The five winning designs illustrating this chapter (all but one tricolors) have several things in common which may prove helpful in checking ideas for flower-show entries.

1. They all expand the meaning and carry out the intent of the schedule.

2. They all show a considerable amount of imagination.

3. They all incorporate material which in some parts of the country would be considered unusual.

4. The coloring featured is either *very closely related,* or shows *maximum contrast.*

5. They all incorporate either closely related textures and a *sharp contrast of color,* or closely related colors and *sharply contrasting textures.*

6. Every arrangement stresses the feeling of depth, taking such full advantage of the third dimension that it is difficult to get an undistorted two-dimensional photograph.

7. Even the one purposefully angular design features a basically planned circular movement.

8. With a little imagination a Hogarth curve is discernible either in the over-all pattern or at the heart of every design.

9. All the designs are well integrated and simply stated.

10. They all stress an ordered movement of growth, rather than a clearly defined, static center of interest.

SEVEN

HOME DECORATIONS WITH A FUTURE

FIXING FLOWERS WITH A FUTURE IS FUN! A FLOWER AR-
RANGEMENT, LIKE A WELL-PLOTTED GARDEN, SHOULD BE
planned for year-round beauty. When a landscape architect specifies
Nandina for a particular location he visualizes white spring blossoms,
feathery green summer foliage, and rich autumn coloring, as well as
brilliant winter berries. Interior arrangements may, with very little extra
trouble, also incorporate this vision of the future.

A single design made for a specific location can happily incorporate
either the jonquils of spring, the roses of midsummer, the brilliant blossoms and fruit of autumn, or the frosty loveliness of outdoor Christmas
scenery. Yet this gratifying continuity is often lost.

A single basic background that is designed to take full advantage of
the decorative possibilities in a room may be used throughout the year.
And, by adding a few fresh flowers, the entire mood may be changed in
a matter of minutes! This type of arrangement is the answer to today's
streamlined living and educated outlook—a common-sense approach to
flower arranging and decorating.

Ideas for using, and reusing, material with a future have been brought
out in several of the preceding chapters. Few people now have time to
spend hours on an arrangement that lasts only a day or two, yet education
has made us too design-conscious to be content with just a bunch of
flowers. Creating a composition that may be used for weeks, months, or

PLATE 25 ►

SEPTEMBER MORN

even years is well worth a few hours of the busiest housewife's time!

Plates 25, 26, 27, and 28 show four different long-lasting designs featuring the ti leaves first used for the dinner party arrangement depicted in Plates 17 and 18.

PLATE 25.

A few days after the dinner the leaves appeared at a flower show as "*September Morn,*" Plate 25. The terra-cotta figurine shyly gazing into a sapphire pool needed little else to carry out the theme. The lining of the terra-cotta container brought out the color of September's birthstone, while the maple burl used as a base repeated the browns of the container and figurine. A Hogarth curve of coral celosia sweeping around the figurine tied the composition together texturally and provided a vivid foil for the semicircle of dark green leaves.

The spiral formed by the ti leaves is quite versatile and the simplest of all designs to construct. In addition to bold foliage such as that shown here, many flowers of varying shapes, including both gladioli and callas, are very effective when arranged in this manner.

The first placement is made on the center back of a round holder. Each succeeding placement, somewhat shortened, follows the curve of the outside needles on the circular holder. The first leaf faces the arranger, and the others turn gradually so that the leaves on the bottom of the spiral face up toward the original placement. This slow turning of the material and the rhythmic shortening of each succeeding stem guarantee success to the least skilled arranger.

After the flower show, "September Morn" took her place on a large modern desk, where she remained until the ti leaves began to change color. The design could easily have been given variety by the simple expedient of substituting other flowers for the celosia. However, the form and color of the celosia changed very little, so it was allowed to dry along with the leaves (see Appendix, item 10).

PLATE 26.

In October, when the ti leaves were showing a touch of tan, a tawny lion replaced the terra-cotta figurine. The celosia in the preceding plate was washed and put away for future use, and sleek variegated

PLATE 26

PLATE 27 ►

aucuba foliage became an accent for the ti leaves. The aucuba was arranged to wind its way through the yellowing ti leaves, directing attention to, and repeating coloring of, the graceful lion at the base of the composition. A base repeating the interesting curves of the lion's feet and body was rubbed with shoe polish and white paint to pick up his coloring and repeat the color and texture of the lichen-covered tree.

The versatility of brown shoe polish has been stressed throughout the book, and many suggestions have been made for its use. It is available to everyone and can often be used to bring completely unrelated elements into close relationship, with very little effort. The addition of a little black or white paint will broaden its field even further.

The base in Plate 26 was the correct shape and size, but its high gloss and deep mahogany hue made it completely incongruous with the rough-textured, gray-toned tree. Steel wool was first used to cut the gloss on the shiny base, then a thin coating of white paint was applied with a soft cloth. When the paint was nearly dry, liquid brown shoe polish was streaked over the base and then rubbed in with a soft cloth. This process blended the white and brown and gave the base a rustic look which made it a suitable foil for the lichen-covered branch.

Before the design itself was changed, yellow zinnias, chrysanthemums, and frost-touched maple leaves, as well as the aucuba, were used for the center of interest in the tropical design.

PLATE 27.

In November flowers were scarce and the ti leaves had dried a delicate tannish chartreuse, so "Mango," with the same paper-wrapped shingle and box used at the original dinner party, again became the center of interest. Eggplant "lilies" (see Drawing V, page 71) replaced the cucumber ones in the first arrangement, and the mystery-filled composition took full advantage of shadows cast by the lamp on the other end of the desk.

Although the sleek purple skins of the eggplant remained intact, the cut portions soon discolored. On the second day the cut ends were dipped in green ink, bringing vivid coloring to the heretofore muted arrangement. (The family immediately dubbed it "The Nile.")

The swirling motion of the leaves was made possible by soaking them in water until they softened enough for molding into the right shape." A strong stick of the proper length was first impaled on a large needlepoint holder, and the leaves were then Scotch-Taped to the stick. The first leaf was attached a few inches below the top of the stick and each succeeding leaf covered the mechanics of the preceding leaf. None of the material required water, so there was no container problem. The needlepoint holder supporting the stick and "lilies" was concealed by two pieces of coal, which also gave the necessary weight at the base of the tall composition.

As the vivid green "lilies" shriveled and changed shape, the name became "Volcano" instead of "The Nile," and finally, "Voodoo." Any bold flowers, such as anthuriums or callas, could have replaced the eggplant; but not until Christmas week did the family agree to a change of design!

PLATE 28.

In December the ti leaves were combined with dark brown lotus pods, feathery pale lavender water canna blooms, and lavender Christmas balls in a bronze usubata. The lower line appears somewhat foreshortened in the two-dimensional photograph, for it reaches well toward the front of the arrangement. The three-point placement plan and the container are the same as those used for the gladioli in Plate 16, the difference being that three groups of material, instead of the three individual gladioli, have been featured. The two small cypress knees at the base of the design conceal crossing stems and help create the illusion of a single growing plant.

For New Year's, gay papier-mâché bells replaced the Christmas balls and water canna. The bells soon gave way to red carnations for Valentine's Day, and then the carnations yielded to a glowing promise of spring as they were replaced by yellow jonquils that had been forced indoors for this purpose. Thus, by replacing the lower line with seasonal flowers, the one purchase of ti leaves became a year-round decoration!

Aspidistra, or even the lowly canna, could be substituted for ti leaves. Permanent background material is all around us; it does not have to be purchased. Often we cannot see the present (much less the future!) of the "weeds" in our own neighborhood, but have a terrific yen for someone else's generally discarded treasures. Even those who are inspired only by "foreign" material need not despair. If your heart is set on palm sheaths when local woods yield only hemlock, somewhere in Florida, Texas, or California lives a flower arranger whose life is full of palm sheaths, but who has always wanted a hemlock bough! Every issue of the *National Gardener* lists State Garden Club presidents, who will gladly supply addresses of arrangers in their locale. One letter is usually all it takes to arrange a swap.

The swap idea has even been set up in some clubs as a money-raising project. Material suitable for use in permanent backgrounds, not avail-

able in the immediate vicinity, is sold at each meeting. The horticultural chairman labels material with botanic and common names, and the arrangement chairman illustrates use of the strange material, thus stimulating the club's flower arrangers and making better horticulturists out of all the members. The plan is fun for everyone, profitable for the club, and educational for both the local group and those on the other end of the swap.

Every locality in these beautiful United States of ours produces some "common" material worthy of a future!

PLATE 29.

Like the basic black dress that fashion designers commend so highly, the type of arrangement shown in Plate 29 is capable of infinite variety. The growing material adds vitality to the design and, even without flowers, presents possibilities of change.

Glads or stock could be substituted for sumacs; the yarrow might be replaced by yellow Dutch irises in the spring and by golden chrysanthemums in the fall. Gold Christmas balls of varying sizes (Scotch-Taped to sticks impaled on the needlepoint holder) curving up through the yarrow heads would be most effective; bright red balls winding down through the sumacs would prove equally interesting. The slightest change gives an entirely different effect! Best of all, if the face-lifting job is done when the arrangement gets its weekly bath, the change does not entail any additional time.

This composition features the same background shown in Plate 22, "Birth of Spring," and most of the material was acquired by swapping with other arrangers. Yet in our part of the country, just keeping things alive is often a struggle. *Every* region produces some material that is unique to some other region.

Opening our eyes to the possibilities about us is a stimulating experience and creates new worlds for the entire family. (The mushrooms in Plate 14 were nurtured by my husband through a two-day hunting trip. His struggles to deliver them intact aroused much amusement, but their enthusiastic reception made treasure hunters out of all three Nimrods!)

The design in Plate 29 demonstrates the advantage of gathering material in various stages of development. Small pink heads of sumac appear at the top of the composition, working down into large dark maroon clusters at the base. The cattails follow the same development cycle. The small ones were gathered in late April and were still encased in their sheaths when cut. They are a vivid chartreuse in this stage of development and retain their color for several days before turning light tan. These particular cattails made their debut at a luncheon with golden water lilies blooming at their feet. The large dark brown cattails at the base of the design were gathered almost two months later and, as a safeguard against shattering, were dipped in a thin solution of shellac before being brought into the house (see Appendix, item 4).

The cypress knee was peeled; then it and the other pieces of wood at the base of the design were rubbed with shoe polish to tie them in with the rest of the composition. The philodendron was placed in a toothbrush container full of water. The container was then taped to a stick and impaled on the heavy needlepoint holder. The sansevieria was rooted in a small vitamin jar filled with damp bird gravel. Both philodendron and sansevieria last indefinitely when given light and water. If the material turns yellow because the light is insufficient, it can easily be rotated with fresh plants each time the arrangement is dismantled for washing.

One of the most important things to remember about this type of arrangement is that the material is washable. Even freshly cut foliage is not at its best when it needs a bath, but cleanliness is doubly important to the subtle coloring of dried material. Nothing that has been properly cured is too frail to wash, and much antipathy toward "dead" arrangements was born in otherwise immaculate houses where an arrangement that has been meticulously dusted *around* for months occupies the seat of honor.

PLATE 30.

Dried material used to have no place in a flower show. However, increased knowledge and experience have brought the realization that flower shows should give workable ideas for beautifying homes, as well as for improving gardens—and such material is a lifesaver to the busy homemaker. For this reason, most well-rounded shows now include at

PLATE 29 ►

PLATE 30

least one class calling for long-lasting arrangements. Many of the
even specify "with easily changed center of interest."

Changing the mood of an arrangement without redesigning the ent
composition is a great timesaver. Plate 30 gives an entirely different v
sion of the background used in preceding plate. Only the central mc
has been changed, yet the two designs have little relation to each oth
The large background is a perfect foil for the five pale pink glads a
chrysanthemums which were substituted for material at the center
the design in the preceding plate. Without the basic design formed
palm sheaths and cattails, dozens of flowers would have been requir
to create as dramatic an effect, and a great deal of time would ha
gone into working out a suitable design.

"Permanent" arrangements should have their faces washed—or bet
still, lifted—for variety, at least as often as venetian blinds are dust
So changing the central motif would entail very little extra work. Wh
properly cured and maintained, plant material is not only colorful, l
practically indestructible—and a far cry from the drab dust catch
of our grandmothers' day.

Almost any seasonable flowers would lend themselves to a compositi
like the one shown in Plate 30—jonquils and forsythia or tulips and re
bud in the spring, roses and larkspur, zinnias, or even dahlias wo
prove satisfactory! It is simply a matter of working out a color sche
and textural relationships in keeping with the room and its furnishin

Backgrounds of this kind, like the walks and trees in well-design
gardens, provide the structural forms for floral accents.

PLATE 31.

It is much simpler to create dynamic arrangements with living pla
material than it is with dried material. Compositions entirely of cu
material depict only past glory and are therefore apt to appear sta
unless very carefully handled. However, such designs may, by follc
ing nature's ordered movement of growth, suggest the coming of spri

Although the arrangement shown in Plate 31 contains nothing l
dried leaves it gives a feeling of suspended animation. It portrays t
pulsing of spring apparent in living trees before the buds begin to sw
in preparation for rebirth.

PLATE 31 ►

The nine handsome *Ficus pandurata* (fiddle-leaf fig) leaves were rescued from a neighbor's trash pile. They were soaked in warm water to soften them and then worked into a three-point design around the same stick that was used in Plate 27. The leaves were attached to the stick in the same manner and in somewhat the same design as the ti leaves, except that this time the urgency of imminent growth, rather than the swirling motion, was emphasized.

The composition features essentially the same three-point design first depicted in Plate 1, which has been stressed throughout the book. The design, based on principles set down for formal Japanese arrangements, receives its vitality from the three distinct planes of depth swinging out from the central axis.

The tip of the tallest line in Plate 31 was, as heretofore, placed immediately over the point where the main stem emerges from the container. Again each succeeding line was made approximately a third shorter than the preceding one, with the middle line reaching toward the back of the container and the lower one pointing over the right shoulder of anyone standing directly in front of the arrangement.

The small cypress knees, first used with the peonies in Plate 2, give stability at the base of the composition. They also further the illusion of a tree growing from a single trunk and spreading above in a naturalistic manner.

PLATE 32.

The celosia in Plate 32, shown "growing" on its own beautifully curved stems, is a composite of many plants. Again the general outline of the original three-point arrangement in Plate 1 was followed, and again the three planes of depth have been stressed to portray the movement of growth. The composition gives a definite feeling of vitality, rather than conveying the nostalgic sadness usually associated with a dead tree.

The beautifully textured stems of celosia dry as satisfactorily as the heavy bloom heads. The curved stems shown in Plate 32 were soaked in warm water to soften them and then forced into shape. They were first pinned together with straight pins to form an interesting design and then glued with transparent waterproof glue. After the glue hardened, the pins were pulled out or cut off flush with the stems. The "tree" has

PLATE 32 ►

been added to from year to year whenever interesting stems became available.

The blossoms change shape after each washing, but can easily be molded back into pleasing forms while they are still damp enough to be pliable. A few pins and a little extra glue is all that is required to repair damages. Fresh blooms, as well as stems, may be added at will.

A composition of this kind is dynamic enough not to become monotonous, and lends itself admirably to the simplicity of today's architectural trends. Once worked out to the homeowner's satisfaction, dramatic streamlined arrangements of this kind can become a permanent part of the decorative scheme.

PLATE 33.

There are flower arrangements with a future even for horticulturists, who are old-fashioned enough to cringe over the floral artist's use of cured material.

Plate 33 shows a living design of philodendron which has been an integral part of a decorative scheme for twelve years. Born of an ex-horticulturist's unfulfilled desire for a garden, the well-balanced soil has never required repotting. The "arrangement" is dusted and given a pint of water once a week; has a bath and receives a teaspoon of plant food once a month; and seldom loses a leaf except to supply material for other designs!

The homemade stand was fashioned of scrap lumber and discarded bricks rescued from the city dump. The foot-square battery-jar container was purchased from the junkyard for fifty cents, and another fifty cents was invested in having the tall jar cut to a more graceful height.

When the dwarf pine tree, for which the setting was originally designed, could no longer take the rigors of apartment life, philodendron was planted at its feet and trained to follow the twisted limbs. The tree finally rotted and another visit was made to the junkyard. This time a whole dollar was squandered on twelve scraps of used copper tubing.

The tubing was bound together with wire and propped up in a tin can of cement. After the cement set, the can supporting the tubes was

placed in the battery jar, and the jar filled with soil. (See Appendix, item 12.)

The design for the philodendron followed the formation of the four-foot pine tree as closely as possible. Two tubes were used for each limb; they were twisted together for solidarity and then bent into shape and cut to the proper length. Small wire bound the tubing wherever necessary to assure firmness.

When completed, the "tree" was painted a soft gray-green, and it is so closely related to the philodendron that a careful examination is required to segregate the green "limbs" from twining plant material. The illusion of a single growing plant was furthered by encasing runners and tubing in coconut fiber where they emerge from the soil, thus forming a naturalistic brown trunk at the base of the design. A few weathered stones beneath the tree completed the garden scene.

The philodendron did not do very well until the greenness wore off of the cement and a regular schedule of feeding and care was worked out. A fluorescent light attached to the back of the stand added drama to the design and made the plant take a new lease on life.

About once a year it is necessary to unwind the runners and rework the design. Round green Twistems inconspicuously hold the runners in place until they become accustomed to the new method of growth.

The philodendron tree makes a very effective background for flowers. Hibiscus, hemerocallis, amaryllis, and orchids are some of the flowers that have "grown" satisfactorily in the tropical setting. Chartreuse Christmas balls and a candle molded in a large mixing bowl also give a familiar friend a new and satisfying use.

This type of arrangement is much easier to take care of than the dust-covered conglomeration of anemic plants usually encountered in planter boxes. The composition does not require diversity of material and is just as effective with easy-to-grow philodendron as it would be with the rarest botanical specimen.

The simply stated design lends real drama to the room either with or without a flower accent.

PLATE 33 ►

SUMMARY

1. Interesting plant material can be used over and over again as a basic background, saving both time and money.

2. Basic backgrounds, like well-designed gardens, should grow out of the site—be in harmony with the particular home.

3. Careful analysis of shapes or patterns best suited to the specific location in the room will simplify selection of suitable background material.

4. Plant material is *washable*. Growing things love rain; a little water will not hurt them after the process has stopped.

5. Several basic backgrounds should be made for strategic locations in the house; even though designs may be perfect, everyone will enjoy a change.

6. Soaking dried material in warm water for an hour makes it pliable and easier to handle.

7. Basic backgrounds should be interesting in themselves and, like gardens, should be designed as a foil for flowers.

8. Arrangements incorporating living foliage or flowers give a promise of something to come and are less static than those composed entirely of cured material.

9. Designs based on a simplified response to growing trees are often dynamic enough not to require an accent of living material.

10. Most successful basic backgrounds feature rhythmic repetitions like those found in nature's ordered movement of growth.

Needlepoint holders come in MANY SIZES,

from thumb nail to giant 8 " and in VARIED SHAPES

or even INTERLOCKING for greater variety and

Ready built to hold water without a container .

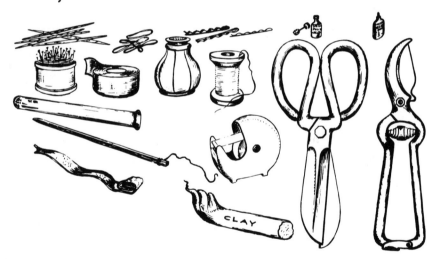

Equipment: Holders and other mechanical aids.

2 Basic containers **+** a few well chosen stands **=**

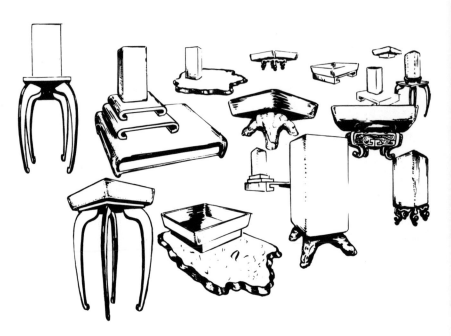

INFINITE VARIETY

Containers and stands.

APPENDIX

PREPARING MATERIAL FOR A FUTURE

1. **WASHING:** *All plant material is washable.* Place the material in a tub of warm water and swish it around gently until the dust is removed. It should then be held upside down and allowed to drain. If the material is to be rearranged, a little dampness will make it pliable and easier to handle. If the material is to be stored, it should be spread out on newspapers and allowed to dry for several hours before wrapping.

2. **STORING:** Backgrounds can be very compactly stored, if they are properly handled. All material should be washed and allowed to drain before storing. Each piece should then be rolled loosely in newspapers to prevent mildew, and packed away for future use. When it is needed again, material that has been crushed out of shape will become pliable enough to mold into new designs if it is soaked for an hour in a tub of warm water. (We live in an apartment and yet have twenty-odd large basic backgrounds stored away. They range from five-foot palm sheaths through banana leaves, pine boughs, century plants, etc., and are all packed in one large basket, suspended from an unused doorway in the kitchen!)

3. **WHEN TO CUT:** Material for curing should be picked during the hottest part of the day, when it has the lowest possible moisture content. The procedure is exactly opposite to that followed for prolonging the life of cut flowers. If plants are waterlogged when gathered,

they are apt to rot; and even if they do not, the color will be muddy. They should never be cut after watering or a rain. A drought year is an ideal time to dry material.

4. STAGE OF DEVELOPMENT: Plant material will give more lasting pleasure if picked *before* reaching its prime, since the maturing process does not cease at the moment of cutting. When pods are picked nature does everything to speed up the maturing process and release the seeds as planned. *From half to three-quarters mature* is usually the most satisfactory stage. Material picked after it has reached its prime will seldom cure satisfactorily.

Pampas grass, thistles, cattails, and other materials that shatter easily should be cut when *less than half matured*. When this type of material is gathered in a later stage of development it should be dipped in a thin solution of shellac to keep it from shattering. One part shellac to one part alcohol will hold material that is not too mature. Too heavy a solution makes it lose its texture and coloring and gives the material an artificial look. The safest procedure is to leave it in the garage or cellar for a week or two after dipping, to be sure it is shatterproof. (Until you try removing a bursting cattail from a carpeted room you don't know what trouble is!)

5. COLOR: Some flowers will change color very little in drying, if gathered in the proper stage of development—*provided* they are picked when quite dry and cured in *darkness*. Celosia (all kinds and colors), goldenrod, liatris (after four years mine still ranges from clear pale pink to deep lavender), bachelor's buttons, straw-flowers, eryngium, thistles, zinnias, and black-eyed Susans are most satisfactory.

Some of the flowers selected may be too mature or too damp, and these will take on varying shades of brown. However, if properly handled, about two third of the material will hold its color indefinitely. Dried arrangements are most emphatically *not* limited to grays and browns.

6. AIR CURING: When moisture is to be removed through atmospheric conditions, the material must have free circulation of air and be hung upside down to avoid a droopy look. It should be tied in small, loose bunches, and hung from a clothesline in basement, garage, or attic —whichever is drier. Freezing is apt to rot the material, so it should be protected from extreme temperatures until *all* sap has evaporated.

If drying space cannot be darkened without cutting out the air, a crocus sack may be tied over the material. In some localities, and with some materials, paper bags may be used; however, they are not recommended for general use since they shut out most of the air. A flour or sugar sack, or any loosely woven sack, may be used for small material; but the cloth should be darkened with coffee or dye, since white lets in too much light. The darker the sack, the less light will penetrate it and the less flowers will fade while drying.

7. **OVEN CURING:** In damp climates, heavy material such as celosia, mushrooms, etc., has a tendency to mildew. This may be avoided by placing the material on several layers of newspaper in the oven. The oven should be turned on as low as possible, just hot enough not to scorch the paper. The oven door should be left open. There will be a musty odor, but it can be minimized by frequent changes of paper. If the material is very heavy, the process may take several days. However, the material may be removed and the oven used for other purposes, since this merely slows up the process and does not otherwise affect the material. When stains no longer appear on the paper, the material is free of moisture and ready for use.

8. **SAND CURING:** In seaside climates, where even plant material that is low in moisture content mildews, sand is the answer. The sand should be sifted and dried in a slow oven for at least twenty-four hours before using. The material is then placed in a cardboard box or baking pan, on about an inch of sifted dry sand. An inch or two of sand should be sifted over the material, and there should be at least an inch between each bloom or leaf. Any number of layers may be cured at the same time, so long as the material does not touch. The impurities and odors are easily baked out of the sand, and it may be restrained, redried, and used indefinitely if desired.

For quick results, the box or pan containing the plant material may be placed in a slow oven. Or, if time is not an element and the climate is not excessively damp, a hundred-watt bulb suspended over the box about an inch from the sand will do the trick. Flowers such as daisies, zinnias, and roses should be placed face down, or face up, on a layer of sand. In this position, sand sifted into crevices will hold the blossoms in shape during the drying process.

Material cured in sand usually retains its color very well, since the process provides total darkness.

9. **BORAX CURING:** If sand is not available, borax is an excellent substitute. Although the process is slower than oven-sand treatment, it is recommended for difficult-to-cure material. Borax is more absorbent than the finest sand and, therefore, gives even surer results. It also has the advantage of not requiring artificial heat during the curing process. A shoe box is excellent for borax curing and may be stored away and forgotten while material is drying.

Anywhere from a week for delicate flowers to six weeks for moisture-filled mushrooms is required for curing. A test bloom near the top of the box should be examined for moisture every week after the first ten days. When the borax no longer cakes around the material, the process is nearing completion. Borax can be used indefinitely, but should be sifted and spread out on newspapers overnight before being stored away or reused.

10. **WATER CURING**: If the climate is not too damp, the most satisfactory method of drying basic background material is to make an arrangement and enjoy it all through the curing process. Simply fill the container with water when the arrangement is first made, and allow it to evaporate after the material becomes sufficiently dehydrated not to droop. Entrancing effects may be obtained by adding a fresh piece of material periodically. (This face-lifting job is easily done when the arrangement gets its weekly bath.) A few flowers will even retain their color when cured in this manner; but as a rule color-curing requires less light.

11. **GLYCERINE CURING**: Material cured in one part glycerine and two parts water will take on a deep, gleaming mahogany hue and remain pliable indefinitely. The secret of success lies in getting freshly cut stem ends into the solution before they dry out. Almost any firm-textured foliage can be cured in this manner; but magnolia, cherry laurel, elæagnus, ligustrums, holly, etc., are especially beautiful.

Arrangements can be enjoyed during the glycerine-curing process even in damp climates where mildew is ordinarily a factor. The color cycle will be completed in from four to six weeks if glycerine is added to the water in the container when the arrangement is set up and the container is kept filled with water until all the glycerine is absorbed.

For an immediate effect (from four to six days) the material should be bone dry when cut. Stem ends should be crushed or split from one to six inches (depending upon the length and general size of the branches) and then plunged immediately into a solution of *hot* water to which proper amount of glycerine has been added. The solution should be carefully watched, since the mixture should not be allowed to fall below the crushed portions of the stems until after all the glycerine has been taken up by the plant. Water should be added as necessary until the oily scum disappears. When this occurs, the glycerine has been absorbed and the curing process completed.

A milk bottle of glycerine solution kept the year round makes a wonderful experimental station. Material can be put in or removed at will, and the project becomes a family one.

During the war when it was impossible to obtain glycerine, both odorless castor oil and mineral oil were tried, with limited success. Any pure, not-too-heavy oil will do the job with some types of material, but glycerine brings best results.

Both pussy willow and spiral eucalyptus treated with glycerine make wonderful permanent line material. They remain pliable indefinitely; never acquire that dry, dead look; and require very few flowers to make an impressive display.

12. PERMANENT LIVING DESIGNS:

(a) *Drainage:* When containers do not allow for proper drainage, charcoal should be used to keep the soil from becoming sour. A pot twelve inches deep requires two inches of charcoal, one inch of coarse gravel, and one inch of finer gravel. In other words, for best results, approximately *one third* the depth of the container should be devoted to drainage material.

(b) *Soil:* One part Canadian peat moss and one part garden loam, with a tablespoon of bone meal for every quart of soil, makes an ideal potting mixture. Peat moss should be squeezed through the fingers to break up any lumps. A dishpan or tub is ideal for mixing. The mixture should be very moist and thoroughly blended. If surplus moisture develops it may be squeezed out and saved for the first watering.

(c) *Watering:* Most house plants do not require water more than once a week. Like gardens, they respond better to an occasional good soaking than to frequent shallow watering. The correct amount of water can only be determined by experiment. Start by underwatering and add a small amount each week until the correct amount is determined.

(d) *Feeding:* A teaspoon of plant food per pint of water once a month is sufficient for most indoor plants. However, blooming plants require increased feeding from the time buds set until blooms are spent. After this they should be given no food and allowed to rest for a month or two.

(e) *Dusting:* An old-fashioned feather duster wielded on watering days will keep plants free of dust. A soft cloth can be used, but this requires more work since the leaves must be wiped on both sides.

(f) *Washing:* House plants should be washed once a month. Usually a soft cloth or sponge and clear warm water is all that is necessary. However, if there is much smoke or grease in the air the job may require washing with soapy water first and then rinsing with clear water. Newspapers or a plastic tablecloth spread beneath the plant will simplify the task.

(g) *Lighting:* If well-cared-for plants drop their leaves or take on a yellowish cast, additional light is usually the answer. Fluorescent lighting is best, but even a regular floor lamp burning near the sick plant at night will often correct the condition.

(h) *Regular care:* Like babies, plants require regular attention. A plant that is overfed and overwatered one month and starved the next will not thrive. Once the correct amount of water has been determined, a regular day — and a regular *time* of day — should be set up for attending to this chore. Right after breakfast on Monday, dust and water; feed and wash on the first Monday in the month — and *stick to it!*

Plants treated in this manner should *never* require repotting.

BIBLIOGRAPHY

Books recommended for further study, listed in the order of their importance to the beginner:

Flowers: Their Arrangement, by J. Gregory Conway. Alfred A. Knopf, Inc., New York.

The Handbook for Flower Shows, National Council of State Garden Clubs, Inc., New York.

The American Colorist, by Faber Birren. The Crimson Press, Westport, Connecticut.

Pleasures and Problems in Flower Arrangement, by Emma Hodkinson Cyphers. Monday Afternoon Club, 114 Prospect Street, Passaic, New Jersey.

Design in Flower Arrangement, by John Taylor Arms and Dorothy Noyes Arms. The Macmillan Company, New York.

Correspondence Course in Japanese Flower Arrangement, by Hazel H. Gorham and Josui Oshikawa. Nippon Bunka Renmei, The New Osaka Building, Uchisaiwai-Cho, Kojimach-Ku, Tokyo, Japan.

Outline of Period Flower Arrangement, by Frances Hannay. National Council Books, Inc., Philadelphia, Pennsylvania.

Munsel Book of Color, by Albert H. Munsel. Munsel Color Company, Baltimore, Maryland.

The Mastery of Japanese Flower Arrangement, by Hoin Koshu Tsujii, translated by Bunsho Jugaku and K. Fujii. Kyu Saga – Gosho Kwado, Soshisho, Kyoto, Japan; and Charles E. Tuttle Company, Rutland, Vermont.

Manual of Japanese Flower Arrangement, by Josui Oshikawa and Hazel H. Gorham. Nippon Bunka Renmei, Tokyo, Japan; and Charles E. Tuttle Company, Rutland, Vermont.

An Approach to Modern Painting, by Morris Davidson. Coward-McCann, Inc., New York.

Japanese Floral Arrangement, by Special Arrangement with Professor S. Ohashi. Yamanaka & Co., Inc.; Nippon Bunka Renmei, Tokyo, Japan.

Art Today: An Introduction to the Fine and Functional Arts, by Ray Faulkner, Edwin Ziegfeld, and Gerald Hill. Henry Holt & Co., Inc., New York.

Japanese Flower Arrangement, by Seido Iwata. Seibikai Floral Art Institute, Tokyo, Japan; and Studio Publications, Inc., New York.

Art in Everyday Life, by Harriet and Vetta Goldstein. The Macmillan Company, New York.

Selected Arrangements of Moribana and Heikwa, by Sofu Teshigahara and Hoin Koshu Tsujii, translated by Mitsuharu Hazhizume. Yamanaka & Co., Inc.; Nippon Bunka Renmei, Tokyo, Japan.

The Japanese Principles of Design in Flower Arrangement, by Kane Shoji and Violet Johnson. The Chiefton Press, Seattle, Washington.